LESLEY CHESTERMAN

A MONTREAL COOK

—

RECIPES AND REFLECTIONS FROM MY KITCHEN

PUBLISHED BY SIMON & SCHUSTER

New York   Amsterdam/Antwerp   London
Toronto   Sydney/Melbourne   New Delhi

To Sylvia and Anthony Chesterman, my wonderful parents, who made every meal memorable.

Introduction

WHAT MAKES A MONTREAL COOK?

There is no way you can grow up in Montreal and not care about food. Whether French- or English-speaking, every person I've met in this city can share a family recipe or name a famous chef. Within minutes of telling anyone I'm a cookbook author, I'm regaled with a cherished food memory, be it a first smoked-meat sandwich, a family sugar shack (cabane à sucre) ritual, or a snack bar of days gone by. It won't take long before I'm told their preference for a St-Viateur or Fairmount bagel. They'll ask for a restaurant recommendation, preferably one where they can bring their own wine.

Montreal is famous for its restaurants. Since 1912, when the Ritz-Carlton Hotel opened the first luxury restaurant in the country, locals and visitors alike have looked on this city as the gourmet capital of Canada. As a former Montreal restaurant critic, I was always happy to discover excellent restaurants all over the country. But that phenomenon is quite recent. While today, the Toronto and Vancouver restaurant scenes are world-class, Montreal's top tables still dominate the national "best of" dining lists.

I've always considered this city a creative hub of new ideas, with our chefs starting more trends than following. And the culinary talent runs deep, with not only Quebecers, but young cooks who come from all over the world to experience our food scene. As someone exposed to all this for decades, and despite Montreal's political and economic ups and downs (and there are many), it's the food that has always kept me tied to my birthplace. But a great food city is not just about its chefs and restaurants. It's also the markets, the boulangeries, the pâtisseries, the butchers, the charcutiers, and the chocolatiers, as well as the farmers, fishermen, and producers.

Quebec is a province famous not only for its foie gras, maple syrup, and blueberries, but also its cheese. With some 700 varieties on offer, 22 of them lait cru (raw milk), Quebec's staggering cheese selection makes us the envy of gourmets Canada-wide. Cranberries, sea urchin, snow crab, lobster, rabbit, guinea hen, deer, seaweed, northern shrimp, scallops, salmon, trout, halibut, eel, walleye—and that's just for starters—are other prized ingredients that grace our top tables.

The beverage scene is equally impressive, with an ever-increasing number of winemakers producing better and better wines despite the challenging climate. Add to that wine importers, agents, and hundreds of schooled sommeliers. And let's not forget the artisan distillers, creative mixologists, and meticulous baristas.

Ultimately, what sets the Montreal food scene apart from any other is the number of people who care deeply about what is in their glass and on their plate. And when you live surrounded by all those Québécois gastronomes, their passion rubs off on you. When cooking at home, you want to brew the best coffee, try to match your favorite bakery's goods, re-create that phenomenal bistro dish, and transform all those magnificent local ingredients to the best of your ability.

Though I grew up surrounded by French speakers, my home was decidedly English. With a mother from a Ukrainian family hailing from Winnipeg, Manitoba, and a British-Irish father, our daily meals early on were certainly more English than French, with influences from all sides. There were some Ukrainian dishes, some English, a few Irish, and yes, the occasional Shake 'N Bake.

Things changed over the years thanks to my mother, who naturally, given her surroundings, was drawn to French cooking. As a young woman in the early '70s, she took cooking classes with French chef Pol Martin and acquired Jehane Benoît's cooking encyclopedia to learn more about authentic Québécois dishes. I even recall driving to Mme Benoît's farm in the Eastern Townships to pick up a rack of her succulent farm-raised lamb. Soon enough, I caught the cooking bug.

Not only did my mother and I watch Julia Child on *The French Chef*, but together we pored over issues of *Gourmet* magazine, reproducing the centerfold suppers or attempting some multilayered dessert. Mom soon left the desserts to me, and by age 19, I was at cooking school. And when not studying the finer points of puff pastry, I was out in my city, soaking up the rich food scene at my doorstep.

More so than in any other North American dining capital, French cuisine is the backbone of Montreal gastronomy, for one main reason: the language. Like many top chefs, cooking students here (including yours truly) began their apprenticeships studying French technique before working under French chef mentors, in Montreal and also in France.

Yet even if the basic style of cuisine and service is undeniably French, a distinct Québécois cuisine has emerged over the years, a melding of traditional dishes with French savoir faire while employing all of those wonderful Québécois ingredients mentioned above. Looking over my repertoire of home recipes, it's clear that that also holds true in my kitchen. But because Montreal is a multicultural city, there are influences from all over, as is the case for most modern cooks. Our cooking is an amalgamation of our surroundings, our heritage, our travels, our memories, our experiences, our likes and dislikes.

This book features a selection of recipes, essays, and recommendations that together form a love letter to Montreal in all its culinary diversity and glory. I hope it will transport you to this wonderful culinary mecca, and inspire you to cook like a local.

When Using This Book

All the recipes were tested using the standard settings on a home oven. For convection baking, decrease your oven temperature by 25°F (about 10°C) or cut your baking time by about 5 minutes. If you are not sure about the variations of temperature in your oven, consider purchasing an oven thermometer. These are inexpensive and extremely helpful.

All eggs are large
All butter is unsalted
All salt is fine sea salt
All pepper is freshly ground black pepper unless otherwise stipulated
All flour is all-purpose unless otherwise stipulated
All sugar is white granulated unless otherwise stipulated
All brown sugar is either light or dark (whichever you have in your pantry)

Whenever possible, I try to purchase humanely raised meats, sustainable seafood, and organic and fair-trade produce. Not only do these tend to taste better, but the people involved in their production are not working under inhumane conditions or with life-threatening chemicals.

PART ONE

TO MARKET!

Montrealers are spoiled with several excellent public food markets, the three largest being Maisonneuve Market in the east of the city, Atwater Market in the west, and Jean-Talon Market a bit farther north. As it's the largest open-air market in North America (and the closest to my home), Jean-Talon is my market of choice. It's open all year round, and because it's located in Montreal's Little Italy, there are lots of excellent food stores and restaurants in the vicinity.

By Friday afternoon, I'm ready to rid myself of all screens and treat myself to an afternoon at the market, when the stands are well stocked and it's quiet before the weekend crowds descend. Browsing the market stalls will always be my favorite way of finding cooking inspiration. I rarely show up at the market with a list, preferring to let the produce dictate my meals to come.

The market peaks in midsummer, when local produce is bountiful, and then carries on until late autumn, when you can pick up the last of the local tomatoes, berries, cruciferous vegetables, and squash. If asparagus is the first sign of Quebec produce in late spring, I'd say October pumpkins are the last.

In winter, the number of market stalls is greatly reduced, but you'll still find plenty of locals crowding the remaining stalls and shops in search of meats, fish, bread, and imported goods. At Christmastime, it's the one-stop spot to pick up not only a tree, but your Champagne, foie gras, turkey, and bûche de Noël.

Before you take me for one of those obsessive ingredient seeker-outers who swears by market shopping, I must confess my weakness for a good supermarket,

where I can arrive, list in hand, to stock up on staples. Inspiration, though, doesn't stop with food shopping. It might also come from a new cookbook, or even a recently acquired pan, knife, or kitchen gadget I want to give a whirl.

On weekends, cooking begins early. I'll make coffee, turn on the radio, (usually Radio-Canada, the French CBC), and, if I'm feeling especially energetic, make something special for breakfast, like muffins or French toast. Saturday's also the day to reorganize the kitchen, or make that big batch of soup or spaghetti sauce for the freezer. Or I might jump into a full-on cooking project, like bread, jam, or pickles. It's also the day I tend to invite people over, for either a family supper or, because it's the weekend, a pull-out-all-the-stops brunch or dinner party.

No matter what the plans for the night, I'll spend a good part of the day in the kitchen.

Breakfast

Breakfast is a perfect example of the dichotomy between the French and English traditions of Montreal cuisine. On one hand, you have your typical Parisian breakfast consisting of coffee and a croissant. On the other, there's the classic North American breakfast of bacon and eggs, hash browns, a slice of tomato, a scoop of fêves aux lard—baked beans. Judging by the crowds at the city's many breakfast restaurants, Quebecers can't get enough of this hearty morning feast, a meal that until quite recently you'd be hard-pressed to find in France. Of course, we can't always eat that way. Montrealers are big on the café-et-croissant combo too. I usually start my morning with coffee and a toasted bagel or, when I'm up for baking, that North American favorite, muffins. (You can get the recipe started the night before, whip the muffins up while the oven preheats, and take your shower while they bake.) And when I feel the need for a maple syrup fix, which is often, I'll make French toast or pancakes.

Montreal's top baristas have become a bit of an obsession of mine. While I'm not as fanatical as they are (grinding, weighing, timing, and fussing over everything from type of filter to provenance of beans), I'm not into popping a pod into a machine or stirring instant coffee into a cup of boiled water either. Happily, there's a middle ground between indifference and fanaticism, and that's good news, because even a few upgrades in your coffee routine can make a world of difference.

Suggestions for fine-tuning your coffee making

Making an excellent cup of coffee is about precision and perfection. The top dogs on the coffee scene use a scale instead of a spoon for measuring, with the ideal ratio for brewing coffee being 1:16 (as in 1g of ground beans to 16g of water, or 15g of coffee per 240ml cup). The ideal water temperature is 201°

to 202°F (93° to 94°C). The coffee must be balanced: neither over- or under-extracted, nor astringent or bitter. Temperature is key: if the water is too hot when the coffee is brewed, it will be bitter. Too cold, and it can taste sour. Purists would never think of adding milk or sugar to their coffee, which would be compromising the integrity of the bean. But unless you are a member of the barista Hall of Fame, such details are a bit much for anyone looking to better their brew. Instead, try these simple tips:

— Use filtered water. A Brita-style filter is ideal for home use.

— Invest in a grinder. The fresher the grind, the more present the aromatics in your coffee.

— As you would buy the best meat from a butcher, purchase your coffee at a coffee house and ask questions, especially regarding the freshness of the beans. Fresh coffee makes a world of difference.

— Do not refrigerate or freeze your beans. Store your coffee in a cool, dark, dry place.

— If using paper coffee filters, opt for bleached ones, as the unbleached brown ones can give the coffee the taste of wet paper bags.

— If you have a scale, use it to measure your coffee.

— Black coffee doesn't necessarily mean strong coffee. It's not in the bean color, but in the brew. You can brew light-colored beans strong, and dark-colored beans weak.

— If using cow's milk for milk drinks, opt for homogenized milk, which has more flavor and more sweetness than 1% or 2%.

— Don't overheat your milk when frothing. Cooler frothed milk tastes sweeter and blends better with the coffee. Use a thermometer to keep it between 140° and 150°F (60° and 65°C). And the froth must be integrated into the whole drink, not just floated on the top. It will separate eventually, but the first few sips should be harmonious.

To make pour-over filter coffee:

— Weigh out your coffee, counting 15g (^{1}/$_2$oz) of beans per cup.

— Grind the beans immediately before brewing.

— Place your bleached paper filter in the cone and rinse the filter with boiling water before adding the grounds to wash away any bits of debris.

— Boil the (filtered) water and let it sit for 20 seconds, then pour enough water over the grounds until just saturated. I wait about 40 seconds longer, then begin the second pour, gradually pouring water over the "bed" of grounds (that's barista talk) and finishing around the edges.

To make cold-brewed coffee:

Too hot for a cup of coffee? Join the hipsters and pour yourself a cold brew. Not to be confused with iced coffee (brewed coffee served over ice), cold brew is a more complex beverage, though easier to make than regular brewed coffee.

The process involves macerating coarsely ground beans in cold water for a few hours, then filtering them out. You can add sugar and milk to the resulting coffee, but it's best to taste it first. Because of its low acidity, cold brew tastes sweeter. This is because the beans never come into contact with heat. The beverage is infused (like a coffee concentrate of sorts), giving it a different chemical profile than traditional coffee.

The secret to successful home-brewed cold-brew coffee is to follow the recipe carefully. Like all coffee, the recommended ratio for cold brew is 16:1, as in for 1L (4¼ cups) of cold water, you'll need about 60g (2oz) of your favorite medium- to dark-roast beans (I use espresso). Be sure to measure before you grind, then grind to "38 to 40," or the coarsest setting on your grinder (the same as for French press coffee).

Pour the cold water over the ground coffee, stir, cover, and refrigerate for 8 to 12 hours, depending on the strength of coffee desired. The coffee should then be strained through a paper filter. It will keep for 4 days, covered, in the fridge.

THE BEST BRAN MUFFINS

MAKES 10 MUFFINS

I love a good bran muffin for its fiber-rich properties, but especially for the taste of the bran paired with the bittersweet molasses. Though molasses has been part of the Québécois diet for centuries, these molasses-laced muffins originated in New England. This batter can be made the night before, refrigerated, and then baked the next morning. Many bran muffin recipes call for adding raisins to the mix. You could, but then we could never be friends.

2 eggs

⅓ cup (75g) packed brown sugar

⅓ cup (80ml) vegetable oil

2 tablespoons molasses

1 cup (240ml) buttermilk

1 teaspoon vanilla

1¼ cups (80g) wheat bran

⅔ cup (90g) whole wheat flour

½ cup (70g) all-purpose flour

¾ teaspoon baking powder

¾ teaspoon baking soda

¼ teaspoon salt

- Preheat the oven to 400°F (200°C). Line a muffin tin with 10 large paper liners or, for crisper muffins, spray with nonstick spray.

- In a medium-sized bowl, whisk together the eggs and sugar until smooth, then blend in the oil, molasses, buttermilk, and vanilla. Stir in the bran and let sit while you sift together the flours, baking powder, baking soda, and salt. Stir the dry ingredients into the wet until just combined (do not overmix).

- Spoon the batter into the muffin cups. Bake for 12 to 15 minutes. Enjoy warm (and don't eat too many, or you may regret it!)

APPLE OATMEAL SPICE MUFFINS

MAKES 10 MUFFINS

These muffins are just the thing in fall when there's an excess of apples
and applesauce in the house. I always have an overflow of cereal in my
pantry too, so I give some of it a good smashing with a rolling pin
and add it to my muffin mixes. The more fiber, the better!

1 cup (140g) all-purpose
flour

¼ cup (35g) whole wheat
flour

¾ teaspoon baking soda

¾ teaspoon baking powder

½ teaspoon salt

1 ½ teaspoons cinnamon

½ teaspoon ginger

½ cup (about 45g)
breakfast cereal or granola

½ cup (50g) rolled oats

6 tablespoons (85g) butter,
at room temperature

⅓ cup (75g) packed
brown sugar

1 teaspoon vanilla

2 eggs

¾ cup (180g) applesauce
(p. 334)

1 apple, peeled, cored, and
grated

½ cup (50g) toasted
walnuts, coarsely chopped
(optional)

- Preheat your oven to 375°F (190°C). Line a muffin tin with 10 paper liners or spray with nonstick spray.

- Sift together the flours, baking soda and powder, salt, and spices into a bowl, then stir in the cereal (or granola) and oats. Set aside.

- In the bowl of a stand mixer with the paddle attachment, or in a large bowl with a hand mixer, cream together the butter and sugar at high speed until fluffy, then blend in the vanilla and then the eggs, one by one, scraping down the sides of the bowl after each.

- Blend in the dry ingredients alternately with the applesauce, mixing until just combined. Fold in the grated apple and the nuts (if using) with a spatula.

- Divide the batter evenly among the muffin cups and bake until puffed and golden, about 25 to 30 minutes. Cool slightly before eating.

- **Note:** To make rhubarb muffins: Substitute the grated apple with 2 stalks diced rhubarb (to make about $1^1/_4$ cups; 180g). Increase the amount of brown sugar to $^1/_2$ cup (100g) and replace the applesauce with $^1/_2$ cup (125ml) buttermilk.

- To add a crunchy topping to your muffins: Combine $^1/_3$ cup (70g) sugar, $^3/_4$ teaspoon cinnamon, and 3 tablespoons melted butter in a bowl and blend together to a sandy mixture. Spoon a couple of teaspoons of the mix over the top of each muffin before baking.

JEAN'S FRENCH TOAST

I never thought anyone needed a recipe for French toast until my boyfriend
made some (heavy on the eggs and nutmeg, ugh!), so this one's for him. You can
make a richer French toast by substituting some of the milk with cream, and you
can fancy it up even more by adding orange liqueur and grated orange
zest to the mix. Then it's good enough to serve for dessert.

2 eggs

1 cup (250ml) milk OR ¾
cup (180ml) milk and ¼
cup (60ml) heavy cream

2 teaspoons sugar

Generous pinch of salt

1 teaspoon vanilla

4 slices Daily Bread (p. 20)
or other good-quality white
bread, challah, or brioche

2 tablespoons vegetable oil
for frying

1 tablespoon butter for frying

Maple syrup for serving

- In a large bowl, whisk together the eggs, milk (and cream, if using), sugar, salt, and vanilla until smooth. Pour into a shallow bowl or pan and lay the bread slices in it to absorb the liquid, turning them over often to soak both sides.

- Heat a frying pan or griddle over medium-high heat and add enough of the oil and butter to thinly cover the surface. When the pan is hot, add the pieces of soaked bread, and turn them over after a minute, or once they are nice and golden. When both sides are cooked, press on the center of the bread to check to be sure no liquid escapes. If it does, flip the bread one more time and fry a few seconds longer. Plate 2 slices per person and serve with plenty of maple syrup.

Note: The French toast can be kept warm on a
parchment-lined baking sheet at 200°F (100°C),
but the longer it's in the oven, the more it will dry out.

DAILY BREAD

MAKES 2 LOAVES

Like many Montrealers, I grew up eating baguettes. Then sometime in the '70s, my mom started bringing home multigrain loaves, which we quickly adopted. But my favorite bread was always Pain Canadien, a tall and light everyday loaf that's brilliant for everything from French toast to croque monsieurs.

1 cup (240ml) hot water

1/4 cup (60ml) cold milk

1 tablespoon sugar

1 1/2 teaspoons salt

2 eggs

2 1/2 teaspoons (1 package) instant dry yeast

3 cups (420g) bread flour

3/4 cup (105g) all-purpose flour

1/4 cup (55g) butter, at room temperature, plus more for buttering the molds

2 tablespoons melted butter or egg wash for glazing

- In a large measuring cup, combine the water, milk, sugar, and salt, then whisk in the eggs. In the bowl of a stand mixer, combine the yeast and flours. Pour the liquid ingredients into the dry and knead by machine with the dough hook on low speed until smooth, about 3 minutes. Gradually knead in the butter a piece at a time, until everything is well blended. Knead 3 minutes more, turn the dough out onto a lightly floured counter, and knead lightly to form a smooth and springy ball. (Or, if making the dough by hand, begin by cutting the butter into the flour as you would when making piecrust, and proceed to make the dough as above, but then knead it by hand on a lightly floured counter until smooth, about 5 minutes.)

- Place the dough ball back in the bowl, cover, and allow to rise until doubled in volume, about 1 to 1 1/2 hours.

- Turn the risen dough out onto the counter, press down to deflate it, and then cut exactly in half (if measuring by weight, you should have about 1lb/450g per piece). Roll each piece into a ball and place on a lightly floured surface, flour again, cover with a dish towel, and let rest for 15 minutes. Meanwhile, lightly butter (or spray with nonstick spray) two 8 1/2 by 4 1/2-inch (22 by 11 cm) loaf pans and set aside.

- **To shape the loaves:** Working with one ball at a time, flip a dough ball over onto a lightly floured counter and, with the palm of your hand, press the ball down to form about a 12 by 6-inch (30 by 15 cm) rectangle. Pick up the sides, lift them off the counter, and stretch outward slightly, then fold the two ends over to meet in the center. Starting at the top end, lift the dough up, fold over into the middle, and press down, then roll the top over to meet the bottom edge of the dough, creating a cylinder shape. Pinch the seam closed and then roll the dough lightly to seal the seam and even it out. Placing it seam side down, transfer the roll of dough to a loaf pan. Repeat the process with the second ball of dough.

- Cover the two loaf pans loosely with plastic wrap or a kitchen towel (I use old shower caps) and allow the dough to rise at least a good inch above the top of the pans (about 45 minutes to 1 hour), then preheat your oven to 375°F (190°C).

- After about 15 minutes, the oven should be hot enough and the dough should be well risen and not bounce back when pressed lightly with your finger. Gently brush the tops of the loaves with the melted butter or egg wash and immediately place in the oven.

    $\longrightarrow$

(continued)

- Bake for about 40 to 45 minutes, or until the loaves are deep golden brown on the top and the sides. Place on a cooling rack, then unmold while still warm and let cool completely on the rack before slicing.

Note: This dough also works well for making hamburger buns. Depending on my needs, I divide the dough to make either 10 buns or 5 buns and 1 loaf.

For Hamburger Buns

- After the first rise, cut the dough into 10 equal pieces of about 3oz/90g each. Let rise on a lightly floured counter, covered with a dish towel or plastic wrap, for 15 minutes. Shape each piece of dough into a ball, and then flatten each ball with the palm of your hand to make it about 3 inches (7.5 cm) across. Place the dough rounds on two parchment-lined baking sheets, cover and let rise until they have doubled in volume, about 30 to 45 minutes. Preheat your oven to 375°F (190°C), brush the dough with melted butter or egg wash, and bake for about 20 minutes, or until deep golden. Let cool completely on a rack before using.

MY JAM GURU,
CHRISTINE FERBER

Jam making was never something I warmed to. My grandmother was a master, but my mother never bothered, and when I worked as a pastry chef, we always used a commercial brand. The one time I experimented with jam making, I bought the most glorious berries and proceeded to ruin them with a vintage recipe that required a ton of sugar and a cooking time long enough to transform the mix from a ruby red coulis to an icky brown sludge. I gave it all away and vowed to never attempt it again.

But as Quebec produces some fabulous berries, there was no denying that making jam would be the best way to preserve their flavor. What I needed was a jam guru. And in France, I found one.

One of the leading destinations for serious gourmets in France is in the village of Niedermorschwihr in Alsace. It's called Au Relais des Trois Epis, and it's the pâtisserie of Christine Ferber, who is not only one of the greatest chefs in France, but the top jam maker on the planet.

Nicknamed "La Fée des Confitures" (the Jam Fairy), Ferber produces 180,000 jars of jam annually. Originally the shop, owned by her father, didn't sell jam at all because everyone in her village made their own, so it wasn't something you'd assume people would want to buy.

The first jam she made was griotte (morello cherry). She put the jars on display in the window, and they all sold that day. Today Ferber makes some 300 varieties of jam, 80 percent of which are produced from fruit from Alsace. Popular flavors include apricot/vanilla bean, raspberry/violet, and rhubarb/passion fruit.

Each variety of jam is cooked in small batches in deep copper kettles. Ferber's technique is to cook the jam quickly with just the right balance of sugar to maintain the integrity of the fruit. Most are prepared over 2 days: a first quick boil to meld the fruit and sugar together, followed by an overnight maceration to draw out all the fruit's juices, and then a second quick boil until the desired consistency is achieved. Her dozen assistants (all women) stir and skim, stir and skim, before delivering each hot cauldron to Ferber for a final once-over before filling, labeling, and shipping the jars the world over.

I only ever follow Christine Ferber's recipes, and here are the two I make most, adapted over the years from her cookbook *Mes Confitures* (Éditions Payot et Rivages, 2020).

ABOUT PRESERVES

My technique for sterilizing jars

— Place clean jars on a rack in a large pot. Fill the jars and pot with water. Cover and bring the water to a gentle boil over medium heat. You can also sterilize jars in the dishwasher, but make sure the jars are hot when filling them.

— Meanwhile, place the flat lids in a small saucepan, cover with water and bring to a gentle boil.

When the jam is ready

— Remove the jars from the hot water, one by one. Pour the hot jam into the hot jars, leaving a 1/4 inch (5 mm) headspace. Wipe the rim of each jar with a clean, damp cloth. Cover with the hot lids and screw on the metal bands until they are fingertip-tight.

— Return the filled jars to the rack in the pot; the water should be deep enough to cover the jars by one inch (2.5 cm). Cover, bring the water to a boil and let boil over medium heat for 10 minutes. (If using large quart jars, process them for 15 minutes).

— Using tongs, remove the jars from the water, keeping them upright, and let them cool for 24 hours. Check that the lids are concave, indicating an airtight seal. Store sealed jars in a cool, dark place. Refrigerate any jars that didn't seal properly and use within one month.

QUICK RASPBERRY JAM

4 generous cups (600g) fresh raspberries

2 cups (400g) sugar

Juice of 1/2 lemon

- Prepare 2 sterilized 1/2-pint jars and keep them hot (I place them in a water bath in a warm oven and fill them with boiling water until ready to use). Place the lids in a small saucepan, cover with water, and bring to a boil; keep hot until ready to use. Place a small plate in your fridge.

- Combine the berries, sugar, and lemon juice in a large pot. Bring to a boil, stirring gently but continuously. Continue cooking at a rapid boil for about 8 minutes, skimming off any foam as it accumulates. Check the set by placing a spoonful of the cooked jam on the chilled plate, and once you can clearly draw your finger through it, it's done. Strain half the jam to remove the seeds, pushing well on the sieve to get as much of the liquid out as possible, then add that liquid to the remaining jam. Ladle the hot jam into the hot jars, leaving 1/4 inch headspace. Wipe the jar rims with a clean damp cloth. Cover with the hot lids and screw on the rings until fingertip-tight.

Fraise
2022
FRAISE
2022

STRAWBERRY JAM

This recipe takes 3 days to prepare, but each step
requires only a minimal amount of work.

2½lbs (1.1kg) strawberries

4 cups (800g) sugar

Juice of 1 small lemon

- **Day 1:** Quickly rinse the strawberries in cold water. Dry them in a towel, hull, and slice in half. In a large ceramic or other nonreactive bowl, mix the berries, sugar, and lemon juice. Cover with parchment paper and let macerate in the refrigerator overnight.

- **Day 2:** In a large pot or Dutch oven, bring the mixture to a simmer, stirring constantly. Pour back into the bowl, cover with parchment, and refrigerate overnight again.

- **Day 3:** Drain the mixture, reserving the juices in the large pot. If you prefer smaller fruit in your jam, chop the strawberries into small pieces. Set the berries aside.

- Bring the syrup to a boil and continue cooking over high heat until it reaches 221°F (105°C) on a candy thermometer. Add the reserved strawberries and return to a boil over high heat. Skim off any accumulated foam and boil for 5 minutes, stirring constantly.

- **To check the set:** Dribble some of the syrup onto a plate, let it cool, and draw your finger through it. If the line holds, the jam is thickened adequately.

- Ladle the hot jam into the hot, sterilized jars, leaving ¼ inch headspace. Wipe the jar rims with a clean damp cloth. Cover with the hot lids and apply the rings until fingertip-tight. After the jars have cooled, check that the caps are concave, indicating a tight seal.

Big Brunches

When I was a kid, my family went out for brunch regularly, but especially on Mother's Day (usually at a revolving restaurant high atop the city center). It was a fancy-dress occasion and the endless array of hot and cold dishes to choose from was my idea of heaven. Since then, I've always loved the smell of Sterno in the morning.

Today brunch remains popular in Montreal, but the buffets and revolving restaurants disappeared at about the same time as the Habs last won the Stanley Cup. Brunch is now a casual weekend meetup where the lines for what are often overpriced egg dishes and watered-down Bloody Caesars can astound. I'm not one for a restaurant brunch, but I'm warming up to a homemade brunch as an entertaining option, especially on holidays to gather with family or friends.

Some of my most vivid childhood food memories are of my mother's New Year's Day brunches. With bacon smells wafting from the kitchen, I recall guests arriving on our snowy doorstep and my sister and me perched at the top of the staircase watching it all unfold. I also remember my mom slaving away in the kitchen the night before, consulting brunch recipes from the latest food magazines.

On the morning of the big event, we were enlisted to stir the eggs in the chafing dish or set up the hot plates on the buffet table. In the early days, my job was also to place cigarettes and ashtrays around the living room. The food was quite elaborate, and I can still recall my mother's brioches filled with mushroom ragout, and the time she tackled braised veal roll-ups, unfortunately skewered with mint-scented toothpicks, which gave the dish a mouthwash-like flavor. Yet despite such occasional mishaps, her brunches were always a success.

What's great about brunch is that it is such a laid-back party; kids should be more than welcome. You can start with coffee and juice and then offer wine (or a good Bloody Caesar) with the food.

Resist the urge to overdo it with brunch. You want a spread, but you don't want too many leftovers. When friends offer to bring something, I'd suggest a green salad, fruit salad, or cheese. What I also like about brunch is the way it can go on for the whole day. Expect people to linger, so choose your guests accordingly. And watch out for those flavored toothpicks.

Beauty's, Montreal

MY TOP BRUNCH SPOT: BEAUTY'S

93 Mont-Royal Ave. West

Montrealers have been flocking to Beauty's Luncheonette, an institution if ever there was one, since 1942. The late and legendary owner Hymie Sckolnick was always there to greet you with a "How are you, dahling?" Today his son, Larry Sckolnick, and his daughters Elana and Julie are there to carry on the family business.

Beauty's has long been the place where Roots-clad couples and families converge to brunch all day long. And nobody does it better. If the décor is strictly *American Graffiti,* the fare is an homage to the city's best feel-good food: the bagel!

I first discovered Beauty's when my sister waitressed there while studying at McGill University. I'd show up with my friends to not only harass her but enjoy the generous portions of cool diner food, including classics like the Mish-Mash omelette, the challah French toast, and the mega pancakes. And then there was the Beauty's Special, that incomparable sandwich made with lox, cream cheese, and sliced tomatoes and onions that says "Montreal" to me as much as Mount Royal. "The Special and the Mish-Mash are our signature items," says Larry Sckolnick, "but the Special is [like] our Big Mac."

Often ordered to share, the Special is usually enjoyed on top of regular breakfast dishes. "People try to re-create it at home all the time but come back telling us it just doesn't taste the same. My mom (the late Freda Sckolnick) made the best," Larry says. "She had the touch."

The coffee is freshly brewed, the orange juice is freshly squeezed, and the bagels come perfectly toasted. Service is fast and friendly, and the atmosphere is pure Montreal. Don't leave without tasting either the rice pudding or Larry's famous banana bread, or picking up some to go.

One word of advice: beware the weekend crush (they don't take reservations). You will usually have to line up for a meal at this Montreal institution, but that's half the fun.

GRAVLAX WITH CARAWAY AND CORIANDER

SERVES 10 TO 15

Smoked salmon is ubiquitous on Montreal restaurant menus and is a definite
brunch fave. Yet as much as I am a smoked salmon fan, I have not yet started
smoking my own, so for now I make gravlax. It takes 2 to 3 days to make,
but the melting texture and fresh sea flavor of gravlax is worth the wait.

6 tablespoons (90g) sea salt or kosher salt, divided

1 2-lb (900g) sushi-grade salmon fillet, skin on, pin bones removed

1 teaspoon caraway seeds

1 teaspoon coriander seeds

1 1/2 tablespoons sugar

1/2 teaspoon freshly ground pepper (preferably white pepper)

2 large bunches dill

- **Wash the salmon:** Fill a large bowl with cold water and add 1 heaping tablespoon of salt. Stir until the salt is dissolved, then add the salmon. Leave to soak for 10 minutes.

- In a small skillet over medium-high heat, toast the caraway and coriander seeds, stirring constantly, until fragrant, about 1 minute. Transfer to a spice grinder or mortar and pestle and grind fine.

- Meanwhile, in a small bowl, mix the remaining salt, the sugar, ground spices, and pepper.

- Remove the salmon from the bath and pat dry with paper towels. Place the salmon skin side up on a clean work surface and sprinkle about half the salt mixture all over it, then rub it in with your fingers.

- Arrange half the dill in the bottom of a rimmed dish large enough to hold the salmon. Place the salmon, skin side down, on the bed of dill and rub the remaining salt mixture over the top and sides of the fish. Reserve a handful of dill for the sauce and place the rest of it directly on the fish flesh. Cover with a sheet of plastic wrap and then place a weight on top (I use a small cutting board with a few cans on top). Refrigerate for 1 day.

- After 1 day, unwrap the salmon, remove the dill, and turn the fillet skin side up. Cover again with the dill, followed by the plastic wrap, and put the weight back on top. Refrigerate until sufficiently cured, 1 day longer for a lighter gravlax or 2 days longer for a firmer, saltier gravlax.

- **To serve:** Unwrap the salmon, scrape off the dill, and place on a work surface. Using a very sharp chef's knife, cut the gravlax on the bias into thin slices. Arrange on blini or pumpernickel or rye bread toast points. Drizzle with the sauce, if you like, and serve.

- The gravlax can be stored in the refrigerator, well wrapped in plastic, for about 5 days after the 3-day preparation period.

DILL-MUSTARD SAUCE

MAKES $^1/_2$ CUP (125ML)

A classic sauce that works wonders at enhancing the salmon.

3 tablespoons white wine vinegar

2 tablespoons coarsely chopped dill

1/4 cup (60ml) Dijon mustard

1 tablespoon sugar

1/4 cup (60ml) canola or vegetable oil

Salt and freshly ground pepper to taste

- In a blender or mini food processor, or using an immersion blender in a small, deep bowl, combine the vinegar with the chopped dill, mustard, and sugar and blend until the dill is very finely chopped. Gradually pour in the oil and blend until a smooth sauce forms. Season with salt and pepper.

EGGS WITH CREAMED SPINACH

SERVES 4

This is my idea of a terrific brunch dish, and if you want to take it a
step further, add bacon and hash browns (recipe follows)

1 5oz (142g) container baby
spinach, washed OR
1 bunch fresh spinach
(about 250g)*

1 recipe Béchamel Sauce
(p. 77)

Pinch of nutmeg

Freshly ground pepper

Salt

¾ cup (45g) grated
Parmesan or Swiss
cheese, divided

4 eggs

2 tablespoons
chopped chives

4 slices sourdough or
Daily Bread (p. 20), toasted
and buttered

***Note:** If using bunch spinach: Fill your sink with cold
water, add the spinach, swish it around, and let it sit for
about 5 minutes. Remove the leaves one by one, tearing
off any thick stems, and place them on a kitchen towel.

- Heat a large pot over medium-high heat and prepare
an ice bath. Add the spinach leaves to the hot pot all at
once and cover. After about 30 seconds, remove the lid
and stir. Repeat the process until the leaves have just
wilted, then transfer them to the ice water to cool. Drain
the spinach and squeeze into a ball to remove as much
liquid as possible. You can even squeeze it out further
in a clean kitchen towel. Chop into small pieces and set
aside.

- Preheat the oven to 400°F (200°C) and butter a
porcelain gratin dish. Once you've made the béchamel,
stir in the nutmeg, as well as a few turns of freshly
ground pepper. Taste for salt, then stir in the spinach
and ½ cup (30g) of the cheese.

- Pour into the gratin dish and bake for 15 minutes (now's
the time to get started on the hash browns and cooking
the bacon if you're making them).

- Remove the dish from the oven and, with a spoon, carve
out four dents in the creamed spinach; crack an egg into
each (you might want to pre-crack the eggs into a cup

→

(continued)

to be sure the yolks are still intact). Season with salt and pepper, sprinkle over the remaining cheese, and bake for another 10 to 12 minutes, until the egg whites are set. Remove from the oven and sprinkle over the chives. You can let it cool for a minute or two before serving.

- **To serve:** Spoon each egg, along with an extra spoonful of the hot creamed spinach, over a slice of toast. Serve with the hash browns and/or bacon alongside if desired.

***Note:** The creamed spinach also makes a great side dish for dinner, just double the amount of spinach.

HASH BROWNS

4 Russet or Yukon Gold
potatoes

3 tablespoons butter

3 tablespoons vegetable oil

Salt and freshly
ground pepper

Cayenne pepper
or hot sauce to taste

- Peel the potatoes and grate them on the large holes of a box grater. Place in a bowl of cold water and swish them around until the water gets cloudy, then drain. Repeat the operation two more times, then place the potatoes on a clean kitchen towel (or a couple of layers of paper towels) and squeeze out any remaining liquid to get them as dry as possible. It will look like a lot of potatoes, but they will shrink down.

- Heat a large frying pan (preferably nonstick or cast iron) over medium-high heat and add the butter and oil. When the pan is hot, add the potatoes in an even layer and sprinkle over a good pinch of salt and some pepper. Count 3 minutes and, with a spatula, fold the potatoes over each other, about a quarter-section at a time, then spread them out again into an even layer. Let cook for a few minutes more, allowing the potatoes to get a deep golden brown and crisp around the edges. If the pan seems too hot, reduce the heat to medium. Keep folding the potatoes over, but give them the time to crisp up each time before doing so. When they're cooked through and golden, transfer to a plate and serve hot.

Note: For an added bit of zip, sprinkle over a few drops of hot sauce.

RHUBARB STREUSEL COFFEE CAKE

SERVES 10

I'm surrounded by rhubarb lovers and come early summer, I make this simple cake, which always scores on the brunch buffet. For a twist, try cardamom in place of the cinnamon, and if you can't find rhubarb, it's also terrific made with baking apples or blueberries. This cake improves with age, so consider making it the night before serving.

Crumble

2/3 cup (90g) all-purpose flour

1/2 cup (110g) packed brown sugar

1/2 teaspoon cinnamon

Pinch of salt

1/4 cup (55g) butter, at room temperature

Cake Batter

1 1/4 cups (175g) all-purpose flour

1 teaspoon baking powder

1 teaspoon salt

1/2 cup (110g) butter, at room temperature

3/4 cup (150g) sugar

2 eggs

1 egg yolk

Pulp from 1 split and scraped vanilla bean OR 2 teaspoons vanilla

1/2 cup (125ml) milk

→

- Preheat the oven to 350°F (180°C) and set an oven rack in the center position. Generously butter a 9-inch (23 cm) round cake pan or springform pan, line the base with parchment paper, and then lightly butter the paper.

- **Make the crumble:** In a small bowl, whisk together the flour, brown sugar, cinnamon, and salt. Using your fingertips, rub the butter into the dry ingredients until the mixture forms small clumps. Refrigerate.

- **Make the cake batter:** In a small bowl, combine the flour, baking powder, and salt. In the bowl of a stand mixer fitted with a paddle attachment, or in a large bowl, with an electric mixer, beat the butter with the sugar at high speed for about 2 minutes, until light and creamy. Add the eggs and yolk one at a time, along with the vanilla, and beat until fluffy, scraping down the sides as needed. Reduce the speed to low and add the flour mixture alternately with the milk. Blend until smooth, but do not overmix.

- **Assembly:** Spread the batter evenly in the pan. Toss the rhubarb (or apples or blueberries) with the lemon juice, sugar, cornstarch, and cinnamon and arrange in an even layer over the batter. Scatter the crumble topping evenly over the top, pinching it as you go to form some larger clumps. Place the cake pan on a baking sheet (this is

→

(continued)

For topping

2¹/₂ cups (300g) fresh
rhubarb stalks, peeled and
cut into ¹/₄-inch (5 mm) dice

OR 2¹/₂ large apples
(300g), peeled, cored,
and diced

OR 2 cups (300g) fresh
blueberries

2 teaspoons lemon juice

1 tablespoon sugar

1 teaspoon cornstarch

¹/₂ teaspoon cinnamon

important to prevent the base overcooking), then place it in the oven and bake until the cake is golden and the center is set, about 60 to 70 minutes. If the crumble gets a bit dark by the 45-minute mark, lay a piece of aluminum foil over the top.

• Cool the cake on a rack, then run a spatula around the sides to loosen it from the pan before unmolding it or unclipping the springform ring. Serve warm or at room temperature.

BOSTOK

I first spotted this breakfast pastry at the famous French pâtisserie Lenôtre, which opened a short-lived franchise in Montreal in the '80s on fashionable Laurier Avenue. Traditionally made with brioche, Bostoks are a bit like an open-faced almond croissant but less messy, easier to make, and, I think, even more delicious.

6 slices Daily Bread (p. 20) or brioche (about 1 ½ inches/3 cm in thickness)

Syrup

⅓ cup (75ml) water

⅓ cup (70g) sugar

Cream

¼ cup (55g) butter

¼ cup (50g) sugar

½ cup (50g) almond flour

1 egg

1 teaspoon vanilla OR ½ teaspoon orange flower water

2 teaspoons all-purpose flour

⅓ cup (40g) slivered almonds

Powdered sugar to serve

- Preheat your oven to 350°F (180°C). Place the slices of bread on a parchment-lined baking sheet.

- **For the syrup:** In a small pot, combine the water and sugar and bring to a boil; set aside to cool. Brush the bread slices generously with the syrup.

- **For the cream:** In a small bowl with an electric mixer at high speed, beat together the butter, sugar, and almond flour until smooth, then blend in the egg, vanilla, and, finally, the flour. Beat until doubled in volume.

- Divide the cream among the slices of bread and spread evenly right to the edges, then sprinkle over the slivered almonds.

- Bake until deep golden, about 30 minutes. Do not underbake, or the bostocks will be mushy. Sprinkle lightly with sifted powdered sugar and eat warm or at room temperature.

BAKED BEANS

I decided to add a recipe for baked beans to this chapter because they're just so popular here in Quebec, especially in sugar shacks and breakfast restaurants. Made with dried navy beans and flavored with molasses or maple syrup and a serious chunk of cured pork or bacon, these beans are slow-cooked overnight, filling the house with the most appetizing smell to wake up to. Baked beans have long been popular in Montreal in establishments known as "bineries," where bines, or fêves au lard, were the specialty. One of the few remaining bineries in Quebec is Montreal's La Binerie Mont-Royal, founded in 1938. Now a popular tourist spot, La Binerie makes great beans, but these might even be better.

1lb (about 2 cups; 450g) dried navy beans

Salt

1 medium carrot, diced

1 medium yellow onion, diced

2 cloves garlic

A few sprigs fresh thyme

1 bay leaf

1/2 cup (125ml) molasses

2 teaspoons Dijon mustard OR dry mustard

Freshly ground black pepper

1/2lb (225g) cured pork or bacon, any rind removed and cut into 1/2-inch cubes

Apple cider vinegar to taste (optional)

- In a medium bowl, cover the beans with several inches of cold water, add 1 tablespoon of salt, and stir. Let soak for at least half a day, but no more than a day.

- The night before you're going to serve the baked beans, drain the beans and rinse them in cold water. Preheat the oven to 250° F (125°C). In a medium bowl, combine the beans with the vegetables, garlic, thyme, and bay leaf. Add the molasses and mustard, with a good pinch of salt and a generous amount of black pepper (about a teaspoon) to season. Then finally, add the pork. Mix well, then pour into a ceramic bean pot or a saucepan with a tight-fitting lid. Bring a kettle of water to a boil and pour over 2 cups (500ml) of boiling water to just cover the beans. Put the lid on the pot (or pan) and place it in the oven before going to bed.

- Cook overnight, for about 10 hours. Ideally, most of the beans will stay whole, or almost whole, and some will melt in the sauce. If you want a tangier taste, add a little cider vinegar.

PART TWO

In Montreal, the seasons dictate the way we eat. The best seasons to enjoy local ingredients in Montreal are summer and early fall. After that, we rely heavily on imported produce. Chefs always put the emphasis on local, seasonal produce, yet I would add that for home cooks, weather is a definite factor in the choices we make come mealtime.

Montreal winters last from December to April. This is the season when we indulge in hearty dishes to give sustenance, perhaps no longer needed for crossing the St. Lawrence River by dogsled, but certainly for shoveling the driveway. During those five long months, I focus on food to keep me warm. I make casseroles and baked pastas, and stop at my favorite butchers to pick up tough cuts of beef and lamb for braising. On weekends, I'll make a big pot of soup and freeze the leftovers for meals to come.

Spring is the shortest season in Montreal, a time when you can be caught wearing boots and a hat when the temperature hits double digits and suddenly all the kids are out walking in shorts and T-shirts, surrounded by the last crusty snowbanks. That transition from cold-weather food to warm-weather food happens so suddenly that, come springtime, I'm ready to throw my braising pot out the window and break the BBQ grill out of cold storage. The beginning of spring in Quebec is also marked by the start of the sugar shack season, when nights are still frigid but the days are warm enough for the sap to begin pouring from the maple trees. I'm already imagining the taste of the balled-up tire (maple taffy) dripping off the top of a popsicle stick.

By the time the warm weather rolls around in late May, we're welcoming local fiddleheads and asparagus back into our cooking repertoire. Markets are packed with Montrealers thrilled to once again be browsing the stands, dreaming up dishes to make with the first produce of the season: morels, radishes, garlic scapes, spring onions, and vibrant greens. And by mid-June, we're gorging on terrific Île d'Orléans strawberries once again.

Come summertime, the weather can quickly turn from mild to hot and humid, when grilling is in full swing and dining usually happens outside, en terrasse. At the market, sweaty customers are lining up for ice cream, while Quebec tomatoes are finally making an appearance. At my house, so do savory tarts, made with either asparagus or tomatoes. It's also time for substantial salads, grilled meats, gorgeous vegetable side dishes, and, for that perfect summer supper, I'll add a bottle of rosé (or several). For dessert, all you do is put those magnificent berries to good use in Pavlovas and shortcakes or simply serve them solo.

And just when you've had your fill of grilled meats and salads, and the nights seem a bit cool for rosé, along comes autumn, my absolute favorite season in the city, when the leaves put on the most magnificent color display and local produce is at its peak. Now the markets are really humming, with plum tomatoes, peppers, eggplant, Brussels sprouts, garlic, squash, melon, autumn strawberries . . . and so much more. We're jamming, pickling, canning, and freezing, preserving all these beautiful foodstuffs for the cold months to come.

By Thanksgiving, the local produce begins to thin out and the nights get chilly. Pools are covered, BBQ grills are placed in hibernation, and that soup pot is back on the stovetop. Apple pies have replaced raspberry tarts, and we're roasting the chicken instead of smoking it atop a beer can.

And so it goes, the great cycle of Montreal appetites, with our warm-weather favorites and cold-weather musts. To me it's as much a part of being a Montrealer as having a preferred bagel spot, cheering on the Habs (no matter how often they lose), and beginning a conversation in French and finishing in English—or vice versa. That climate-adapted cooking is something we share not only with all Quebecers and Canadians, but with anyone who relishes the comfort of a hot bowl of soup on a cold winter night.

Soups, Salads, and Light Meals

WEEKEND SOUP

My mom made this soup every weekend when she cleaned out the refrigerator crisper.
We loved it so much that we'd often eat half of it before it had finished cooking. It's
really just a cream of vegetable soup, but I still see it on French restaurant menus
and order it whenever I do. I like this soup as is, or with a sprinkling of
chopped parsley or, even better, croutons sautéed in garlic butter.

2 medium yellow onions

2 branches celery

4 medium carrots

1 large Yukon Gold or
Russet potato

½ small rutabaga

1 small bunch broccoli

1 small head cauliflower

¼ cup (55g) butter

Salt and pepper to taste

6 to 8 cups (1.5 or 2L)
chicken or vegetable broth

¼ to ½ cup (60ml to
120ml) whipping cream

- Peel the onions, celery, and carrots and chop them into
  a small dice. Peel the potato and rutabaga and cut into
  cubes. Slice the broccoli and cauliflower into small
  florets. Slice the tops of the broccoli stalks into rounds,
  but discard the tough bases.

- In a large soup pot or Dutch oven, melt the butter over
  medium-high heat. Add the onions, stir in a large pinch
  of salt and pepper, cover, and cook until translucent,
  stirring from time to time. Uncover, add the celery,
  carrots, potato, and rutabaga, and continue to cook
  until the vegetables are softened but not colored,
  turning down the heat to medium if needed.

- Add the broccoli and cauliflower, stir everything
  together, and then pour over enough stock to cover the
  vegetables. Bring to a boil, reduce to a simmer, and
  cook, partially covered, for about 20 minutes, or until
  all the vegetables are cooked through. Remove from the
  heat and let cool. The soup is already delicious as is.

- When the soup has cooled, purée, using either a
  standard blender or hand blender. Pour back into the
  pot, bring to a boil, and stir in as much or as little cream
  as you like. Bring back to a simmer, taste to adjust the
  seasonings, and serve.

Note: This recipe should be used as a guideline, so feel
free to add any leftover vegetables, in any combination
you would like. I like leek in here too, but mushrooms
and squash don't really fit this flavor profile.

BORSCHT

SERVES 6

My Ukrainian grandmother was a great borscht maker, though I remember hers as more of a vegetable soup than a beet soup. Served in large portions with slices of buttered rye bread alongside, it's hearty enough for a meal, but smaller bowls, served cold even, make for an elegant appetizer. And its bright pink color is fabulous.

3 medium beets (about 300g), peeled

3 tablespoons butter

1 medium onion, peeled and diced

2 medium carrots, peeled and sliced into rounds

2 stalks celery OR 1/2 celery root, peeled and diced

1 teaspoon allspice OR caraway seeds

1 bay leaf

6 cups (1.5L) beef or vegetable stock

2 medium potatoes, peeled and diced

1/2 small cabbage (red or green), thinly sliced

4 garlic cloves, peeled and crushed

2 tablespoons cider vinegar

1 teaspoon sugar

Salt and freshly ground pepper

Sour cream and fresh dill and/or chives to serve

- Dice 2 of the beets and grate the other.

- Melt the butter in a large frying pan, add the onion, and cook over medium-low heat for 5 minutes.

- Add the carrots, celery, diced beets, and spices and mix well to coat with the butter. Cook for a further 10 minutes, adding a little stock to prevent the mixture from drying out.

- Add the potatoes, pour in the rest of the stock, and simmer for 15 minutes. Then add the cabbage, garlic, and grated beet. Cook until all vegetables are tender, about 10 minutes.

- Add the vinegar, sugar, and salt and pepper to taste and mix well.

- Serve the soup in bowls, topped with a dollop of sour cream and sprinkled generously with dill and/or chives.

PEA SOUP

SERVES 6

I love pea soup, a classic here in Quebec and hugely popular in my house. But what really makes for a next-level pea soup is using the stock left over after poaching a large bone-in ham. If you have some, excellent; if not, rest assured it's even great made with water.

2 tablespoons butter

2 carrots, peeled and diced

2 celery stalks, diced

1 medium yellow onion, diced

2 large garlic cloves, peeled and minced

2 cups (400g) dried yellow split peas or mixed split peas for soup

4 cups (1L) chicken, turkey, ham, or vegetable stock + 6 cups (1.5L) water

OR 10 cups (2.5L) water

2 bay leaves

1 teaspoon dried savory (if you like it)

A few sprigs fresh thyme or 1 teaspoon dried

Salt and freshly ground pepper to taste

2 cups (about 250g) diced country ham

Extra-virgin olive oil for serving

- In a large Dutch oven, melt the butter over medium-high heat, then add the carrots, celery, and onion. Reduce the heat to medium and stir until softened, then add the garlic and cook until the onions just start to take on a golden hue, about 8 minutes in all.

- Stir in the split peas, along with the stock and 5 cups of water (or 9 cups water) and add the bay leaves, savory (if using), thyme, and salt and pepper. Bring to boil, reduce to a simmer, partially cover, and cook for 1 hour, stirring every so often.

- Stir in the ham and cook for a further 30 minutes. The soup is done when the peas are completely cooked through. Adjust the seasonings and add more water if the consistency seems too thick.

- Discard the bay leaves and thyme sprigs and serve hot. I add a drizzle of olive oil to the soup and pair it with large slices of toasted country bread spread thickly with butter or rubbed with garlic.

Note: The best pea soup I ever ate was the one at the Cabane au Pied de Cochon where it's served with small pieces of foie gras. If you have foie gras handy, forget the ham here and add small cubes of lightly salted, raw foie gras in the serving bowls before you pour in the soup, like they do. It's crazy delicious.

ABOUT BÉCHAMEL

The milk-based sauce known as béchamel is one of the mother sauces of French cuisine. Thickened with a roux (a cooked paste made of equal amounts of butter and flour), this sauce has been in use since the 18th century in France and, some claim, as early as the 16th century in Italy. As for the name, that is often credited to a certain marquis by the name of Louis de Béchamel, who apparently suggested to his cook that a sauce be made with a base of milk rather than cream. The first written recipe for it dates to 1733 in *Le cuisinier moderne* (*The Modern Cook*), by Vincent Lachapelle. Béchamel is not strictly French and is referred to as "besciamella" in Italian cuisine, "besamel" in Greek, or plain ol' white sauce in the U.S.

Béchamel may have quite the impressive pedigree, but the truth is it, like most of its fellow mother sauces, fell out of favor in the 1970s with the onset of Nouvelle Cuisine. You'd have a tough time finding an innovative chef today who would sing its praises. That said, béchamel has remained an asset to the home cook and is key to many classic recipes, from endives gratinées to chicken à la king. Stir some grated Cheddar, Gruyère, Emmental, or even Parmesan into your béchamel, and you're looking at a mornay sauce, perfect for a mac and cheese. When my kids were young, I used that very sauce to zuzz up cauliflower and broccoli or to add to spinach to make a lighter version of that steak-house favorite, creamed spinach. When assembling a fancy lasagna, I spread a béchamel or a Parmesan-enriched mornay sauce flavored with roasted garlic between the layers.

Not only does béchamel add lusciousness to dishes like moussaka and lasagna, but it can also be used instead of cream to smooth out or thicken sauces or soups.

In cooking school, we made pots of béchamel and always seasoned it with a clove-studded onion, parsley stems, and a bay leaf, but feel free to flavor it to your liking. We'd pour it into shallow pans and keep it refrigerated to have on hand, which you can easily do at home.

I use it in this book for the macaroni and cheese, croque monsieur, shepherd's pie, and creamed spinach, so here is my master recipe to cover them all.

BÉCHAMEL SAUCE

To avoid lumps in your sauce, it's important that the milk (or cream and
milk mixture) is cold and the roux is hot. And be sure to stir constantly,
as béchamel tends to stick to the bottom of saucepans.

3 tablespoons (45g) butter

3 tablespoons (25g) all-purpose flour

2 cups (500ml) milk

OR 1 1/2 cups (375ml) milk and 1/2 cup (125ml) whipping cream

1/2 teaspoon salt

Freshly ground pepper to taste, preferably white (for color)

Pinch of nutmeg

- In a medium saucepan, melt the butter over medium-high heat. Add the flour and with a whisk, stir vigorously for a good 30 seconds. While whisking, slowly pour in a cup of milk, and continue whisking to remove any lumps. Add the remaining milk (or milk and cream) a little at a time, whisking constantly, until the mixture is smooth and creamy. Stir in the salt, pepper, and nutmeg. Reduce the heat to medium-low and simmer for 5 minutes.

- Use immediately, or pour into a shallow dish, cover with plastic wrap pressed against the surface, and refrigerate for up to a week.

CROQUE MONSIEUR

SERVES 4

A croque monsieur is just a fancy French ham and cheese sandwich. But the authentic ones include béchamel sauce, making for a far more velvety texture.

8 1-inch-thick (2.5 cm) slices Daily Bread (p. 20) or other good-quality white bread

1 cup (250ml) Béchamel Sauce (p. 77)

1 cup (75g) grated Swiss cheese (such as Gruyère or Emmental)

8 to 12 slices ham

- Preheat the oven to 425°F (210°C). Prepare a foil-lined baking sheet.

- Lightly toast the bread (my preference, but it's not necessary) and place the slices on the baking sheet.

- Whisk the béchamel until smooth and then whisk in $^3/_4$ cup cheese. Spread about a tablespoon of the sauce onto 4 slices of bread (make sure to spread it right to the corners) and then top each with 2 or 3 slices of ham. Spread another tablespoon of béchamel over the ham on each toast and then top with the second pieces of bread, pressing down lightly. Spread the remaining béchamel equally over the tops of the 4 sandwiches, and then sprinkle over the remaining cheese.

- Bake until the tops are golden and bubbling, about 15 minutes. Let cool slightly before eating.

TOMATO GALETTE

SERVES 6

There comes a time every summer when my enthusiasm for local tomatoes gets the best of me and I end up with more than I can use in salads and sandwiches. That's where this tart comes in. I always give the tomatoes a light roast beforehand to intensify the flavor.

1 1/2lbs (675g) tomatoes (preferably heirloom and multicolored)

Salt and freshly ground pepper

Pinch of sugar

About 2 teaspoons fresh thyme leaves

About 3/4lb (350g) flaky pie dough, store-bought or homemade (p. 327)

Filling

1 cup (225g) mascarpone cheese or cream cheese

1/2 cup (30g) finely grated Parmesan cheese

1/4 cup (60ml) crème fraîche or whipping cream

2 egg yolks

1/2 teaspoon salt

1/2 teaspoon freshly ground pepper

2 tablespoons snipped basil and chives (or other fresh herbs of your choice)

1 tablespoon olive oil

1 egg, beaten, to glaze the pastry

- Preheat the oven to 250°F (120°C) and prepare a parchment-lined baking sheet. Slice the tomatoes into 1/4-inch-thick (5 mm) rounds, lay them on the baking sheet, and sprinkle over a generous pinch each of salt and pepper, the pinch of sugar, and the thyme leaves. Roast in the oven for about 1 hour, or until half dehydrated, keeping a close eye on the tomatoes toward the end to make sure they don't color. Let cool on the baking sheet.

- Meanwhile, prepare the tart base: Line a baking sheet with parchment paper. Roll out the dough into a 15-inch (38 cm) circle, 1/8-inch-thick (3 mm). Roll it up around the rolling pin and unroll it onto the baking sheet. Chill for 30 minutes.

- Increase the oven temperature to 400°F (200°C) and place a rack in the lowest position. Prepare the filling by whisking together all the ingredients except for the olive oil and the egg.

- **To assemble:** Trace a 12-inch (30 cm) circle lightly in the center of the dough and spread the filling in an even layer over it. Using a spatula, lift up the roasted tomato slices and place them in a decorative spiral over the filling. Fold the edges of the dough over to partially enclose the filling and then lightly press down on the pleats to keep the crust from rising when baking. Drizzle the tomatoes with the olive oil and brush the edges of the pastry with the beaten egg.

- Place the tart in the oven and immediately lower the temperature to 375°F (190°C). Bake the tart for around 45 to 50 minutes, or until the pastry is golden and the filling is beginning to brown between the tomatoes. Let cool slightly and serve warm, in wedges.

ASPARAGUS AND RICOTTA TART

SERVES 6

Asparagus is among the first local produce to show up around Mother's Day
in Quebec. After I've had my fill of steamed, grilled, and stir-fried asparagus,
I'll make this chic tart. Paired with a simple green salad and a glass
of Sancerre, it makes a delightful and very glamorous lunch.

About ¾lb (350g) flaky
pie dough, store-bought or
homemade (p. 327)

1 bunch (about 10oz/300g)
asparagus

Salt

1 cup (250g) ricotta

1 egg

1 egg yolk

½ cup (30g) finely grated
Parmesan cheese

2 teaspoons fresh thyme
leaves, finely chopped

2 teaspoons finely grated
lemon zest

¼ cup (60ml) whipping
cream

½ teaspoon freshly ground
pepper

- Roll out the dough to line a 9-inch (23 cm) round or square tart pan and fit it into the pan. Refrigerate for at least 30 minutes.

- Preheat the oven to 400°F (200°C) and blind-bake the tart shell (p. 268).

- Meanwhile, cook the asparagus: Prepare a pot of boiling salted water and set up an ice bath. Cut off or snap off the woody bases of the asparagus stalks, and rinse them well under cold water. Plunge the asparagus a handful at a time into the boiling water, allowing 3 minutes (for al dente cooking), then plunge into ice water. Drain the asparagus, transfer to a paper towel on a plate, and refrigerate.

- **For the filling:** In a medium bowl, mix all the remaining ingredients with a fork.

- When the tart base is blind-baked, spread the cheese mixture over it, getting it well into the corners. Garnish generously with rows of the asparagus and season the top with salt and the pepper.

- Place in the oven, then immediately reduce the temperature to 350°F (180°C).

- Bake for 25 to 30 minutes, or until the filling begins to puff up around the edges. Remove from the oven and cool a bit before slicing and serving.

MY LIPP SALAD

SERVES 4

I first tasted this salad 25 years ago in Paris at the famous Brasserie Lipp
and was charmed by its simplicity (there are so few ingredients), but more so its
complexity of flavors and textures. At Lipp, they serve it in individual bowls,
but I like making it for a crowd, arranged on a platter, as an appetizer or
for lunch, with nothing but a few slices of baguette alongside.

8 red beets (about
1.6lbs; 750g)

1 tablespoon olive oil

Salt

Classic Vinaigrette (recipe
follows)

About 1/2lb (225g) thin
green beans (haricots verts)

4 large handfuls of mâche
(lamb's lettuce) and/or oak
leaf lettuce, washed and
spun dry

1/4lb (125g) goat cheese
(dry enough to crumble)

1/2 cup (50g) walnuts
and/or pistachios

- Preheat your oven to 400°F (200°C). Slice off the top and the root end of each beet. Cut off two large sheets of aluminum foil and place them on top of each other in a cross pattern. Place the beets snugly in a single layer in the middle, drizzle over the olive oil, sprinkle over some salt, and then wrap in the foil to make an airtight package. Place on a baking sheet and roast for about 60 minutes, or until the beets can easily be pierced with a knife.

- Let cool in their wrapping, then peel away the skins. Cut the beets into large cubes, place in a bowl, and stir in 3 tablespoons (45ml) vinaigrette; cover and refrigerate until ready to serve.

- Top and tail the beans and then blanch in boiling salted water for 2 minutes (you want them al dente). Immediately plunge them into ice water to cool. Drain and roll up in a sheet of paper towels to dry.

- Assemble the salad on a large platter or in bowls: Place the lettuce on the platter or divide among individual bowls. Place the beets over the lettuce, add the green beans, crumble over the goat cheese, sprinkle over the nuts, and then drizzle over the remaining vinaigrette. Serve immediately.

CLASSIC VINAIGRETTE

If you have walnut oil on hand, you can use it in place of one of
the oils below, depending on your taste. Used on their own or in a
dressing, nut oils add a rich and buttery flavor—with just a hint
of bitterness—to salads and vegetable dishes.

1 shallot, minced

3 tablespoons red wine or
sherry vinegar

Salt and freshly ground
pepper

1/2 teaspoon Dijon mustard

1/4 cup (60ml) extra-virgin
olive oil

1/4 cup (60ml) vegetable oil

- Place the shallot in a small bowl and add the vinegar
  and a large pinch each of salt and pepper. Whisk to
  dissolve the salt, then blend in the mustard, followed
  by both oils. This vinaigrette can also be shaken up in
  a jar. Refrigerate for up to a week.

PINK SALAD

SERVES 4

I considered calling this a Russian salad because of the beets, dill, and dressing, but my real inspiration came from The Mike Bossy Restaurant. Owned by the late, great Canadian hockey player who made his name with the New York Islanders, this Montreal steakhouse only lasted for a couple of years, but the salad they served lives on in my memory. I added a few flourishes of my own, substituting chicken for their chopped egg (though I like both), and mixing in the radicchio for pizzazz. I had to do some guessing about the dressing. But what I remember most was that they tossed it all over a bowl of ice, which made the colorful salad especially fresh and crunchy.

1 cup (165g) cooked chickpeas

½ small red onion, finely chopped

1 cup (about 150g) pieces chopped, cooked chicken

OR 2 hard-boiled eggs, chopped

4 large cooked beets (about 600g; see p. 84), diced

2 heads Little Gem lettuce or 1 romaine heart, sliced into 1-inch (2.5 cm) pieces.

½ small head radicchio, ripped into large pieces

About ¼ cup chopped dill (or parsley), plus (optional) sprigs for garnish

Russian Dressing (recipe follows)

- If possible, place your salad bowl over a large bowl of ice to chill it, or place in the freezer (or at least the fridge) for 15 minutes before tossing the salad.

- When ready to serve, toss everything except the dressing together, then pour on the dressing and toss until the salad is well coated and it turns pink throughout. Serve immediately, with extra dill sprigs over the top, if you like.

RUSSIAN DRESSING

MAKES 1/2 CUP (125ML)

1/2 small onion

1/4 cup (60g) mayonnaise, homemade or store-bought (I use Hellmann's)

1 tablespoon chili sauce (or ketchup)

1 teaspoon Sriracha or other hot sauce

2 teaspoons bottled horseradish

1/2 teaspoon Worcestershire sauce

1/4 teaspoon salt

Pinch of paprika

• Grate the onion on a Microplane grater into a small bowl, then whisk in the remaining ingredients. For a more pourable consistency, you can whisk in a tablespoon of hot water. Refrigerate for up to a week, until needed.

NOW THAT'S A SALADE NIÇOISE!

SERVES 6 AS AN APPETIZER OR 4 AS A MAIN COURSE

Like Caesar salad, Salade Niçoise is one of the most used and abused restaurant dishes out there. Assembled with indifference, it's as dreary as they come. But when it's made with love, you're looking at one of the sexiest salads around, especially in summer, when all its components are at their local-produce peak. For a casual lunch, make it the authentic way with canned tuna. But for a dinner party main course, I go for grilled sustainable fresh tuna. This salad can be served individually plated or on a large platter.

Vinaigrette

1 tablespoon Dijon mustard

2 garlic cloves, chopped fine

2 to 3 anchovy fillets, minced

¼ cup (60ml) white wine vinegar or lemon juice

1 teaspoon salt

1 teaspoon freshly ground pepper

1 cup (250ml) olive oil OR ½ cup (125ml) olive oil and ½ cup (125ml) vegetable oil

Salad

8 small new potatoes (red and/or white)

2 tablespoons chopped chives

¾lb thin green beans (haricots verts), trimmed, OR 1lb thin asparagus, woody ends snapped off

2 red bell peppers, roasted and peeled

- **Prepare the vinaigrette:** In a lidded jar, combine the mustard, garlic, anchovies, vinegar (or lemon juice), salt, and pepper. Cover and shake until well blended. Add the oil (or oils), cover again, and shake until smooth. Set aside.

- **Prepare the potatoes:** Place the potatoes in a saucepan, cover with cold salted water, and bring to a boil over high heat. Cover, reduce the heat to low, and simmer for about 20 minutes, or until the potatoes are tender. Drain and set aside until cool enough to slice, then cut in half. Toss with a few large spoonfuls of the vinaigrette as well as the chives. Cover and set aside.

- **Prepare the beans (or asparagus):** Blanch the beans (or asparagus) in boiling salted water until al dente, then immediately drain and immerse in ice water. Drain and set on a paper towel to dry.

- **Prepare the peppers and tomatoes:** Slice the roasted peppers in half, remove the seeds and membranes, and then slice into thin strips. Slice the tomatoes in half.

- If you're serving this on a hot day, chill all the prepared vegetables until ready to serve.

About 20 cherry tomatoes

2 8oz (227ml) cans olive-oil–packed tuna, drained OR 2 fresh tuna steaks (about 3/4-inch-thick; about 1lb in all)

Salt and freshly ground pepper

A few handfuls of frisée or Little Gem lettuce leaves

3 hard-boiled eggs, peeled and quartered

1 medium red onion, sliced thin

1 cup best-quality olives, preferably Niçoise

About 1 cup (loosely packed) basil leaves, ripped into large pieces

- **If using fresh tuna:** About 20 minutes before serving, heat a grill pan over high heat for about 3 minutes, or until very hot. Sprinkle the tuna with salt and pepper, then brush lightly on both sides with a bit of the vinaigrette. Grill the tuna steaks until they are lightly browned on the outside and cooked until rare on the inside, about 2 minutes on each side. Place on a plate to cool slightly. When the tuna is lukewarm, slice into strips or large chunks.

- If you would like to grill the beans (or asparagus), place on the hot grill pan until lightly charred. Set aside.

- **To serve:** You can either arrange all the ingredients grouped together on a platter or toss everything in a large salad bowl, or you can plate the salad individually: Place a small handful of lettuce leaves on each plate. Divide the green beans (or asparagus) among the plates, along with the eggs, and repeat the process with the tomatoes, peppers, and potatoes to fill up the empty spaces. Scatter the sliced onion over the top of all the ingredients, followed by the olives, and finally the basil leaves. Place the canned tuna or cooked fresh tuna strips (or pieces) in the center and spoon over enough vinaigrette to season the salad and the fish but not drown it. Serve immediately.

Everyday Dinners

SPAGHETTI WITH VEAL AND SAUSAGE RAGÙ

SERVES 6 TO 8

I developed this recipe with my friend and former cooking student chef Michele Forgione. Mike has long been my go-to for Italian recipe advice as he, along with partner Stefano Faita, owns and operates three of Montreal's best Italian restaurants: Impasto, Gema, and Vesta. I serve this ragù with spaghetti, but any pasta shape will do. It's also worth doubling the sauce recipe and freezing some to have on hand for weekday dinners.

For the sauce

MAKES 6 CUPS

1 tablespoon olive oil

1 lb (450g) Italian sausages (spicy or not), removed from casings

1 lb (450g) ground veal or beef

1 medium onion, red or yellow

1 stalk celery

1 medium carrot

2 tablespoons tomato paste

1 ½ cups (375ml) white wine

1 28oz (796ml) can San Marzano tomatoes

1 large garlic clove, peeled

1 or 2 Parmesan rinds (optional)

1 lb (450g) spaghetti or other pasta

- In a large frying pan or Dutch oven, heat the olive oil over medium-high heat. Add the sausage, breaking it up into small pieces with a wooden spoon as you go, followed by the ground veal (or beef), breaking it up the same way. Then stir while sautéing, breaking up any large clumps of the meat with your spoon as you go.

- Meanwhile, chop the vegetables fine, either by hand or in a food processor. Once the meat is deeply and evenly browned, stir in the vegetables and sauté for a few minutes more.

- Push the meat mix to one side of the pan and add the tomato paste to the other. Stir to cook the paste for a minute and then blend it into the rest. Pour in the wine, stir, and let it reduce until there's almost none left.

- Meanwhile, drain the tomatoes, reserving the juices, and then fill the can halfway with water (to get the last of the tomato juices). When the wine has reduced adequately, stir in the tomato juices and the water in the can, then add the tomatoes by squeezing them in your hand over the pan before dropping them in. Give the whole thing a big stir and add the garlic clove and

→

(continued)

For the sauce

To finish the dish
6 tablespoons (80g) butter

Grated Parmigiano-
Reggiano

Parmesan rinds (if using). Reduce the heat to medium and simmer for 30 minutes, or until the ragù is the texture of porridge, loose but not runny. Remove the garlic clove to a plate, crush it to a paste with the back of a fork, and stir it back into the sauce.

- Boil the spaghetti according to the manufacturer's instructions; set aside a cup of the pasta cooking water and drain the pasta.

- **To serve:** Heat the butter in a large frying pan and add three-quarters of the sauce. Stir well, then add the spaghetti (or other pasta). Stir vigorously, adding a bit of the pasta water if needed. You want your sauce to coat and glisten on the pasta without it being too dry or soupy. Add more of the sauce if you like. Off the heat, stir in a handful of Parmesan, then transfer to a large serving bowl or plate individually, and serve with more cheese alongside.

MAX'S MAC 'N' CHEESE

SERVES 8

My older son, Max, is a macaroni and cheese lover and requests it on every special occasion. I'll often say yes, because despite the calorie count on this one, homemade macaroni and cheese is one of life's great pleasures. It's perfect for a family meal with a salad, but serve it as a side dish at your next fancy dinner party, and watch your guests lap it up.

For the topping

2 tablespoons butter, plus more to butter the dish

1 cup (120g) breadcrumbs (not too fine) or panko, or a mixture

½ cup (30g) grated Parmesan cheese

½ cup (50g) grated Cheddar cheese

For the macaroni

½ cup (110g) butter

½ cup (70g) all-purpose flour

5 cups (1.25L) milk

1 cup (250ml) whipping cream

1 teaspoon salt

1 teaspoon dry mustard

1 teaspoon Worcestershire sauce

½ teaspoon garlic powder

½ teaspoon freshly ground pepper

- **For the topping:** In a skillet over medium heat, melt the butter, add breadcrumbs (and/or panko), and toss to coat well with butter. Remove from the heat. In a bowl, mix the two cheeses together, and when the breadcrumbs have cooled, mix them in.

- Preheat the oven to 375°F (190°C). Butter a 9 by 13-inch (23 by 33 cm) baking dish and set aside.

- **For the macaroni:** Make the béchamel: In a large saucepan, melt the butter over medium-high heat. Whisk in the flour and stir vigorously for about 30 seconds. While whisking, slowly pour in a cup of milk and whisk until there are no lumps. Whisk in the remaining milk and cream in a thin stream until the mixture is completely smooth. Stir in the salt, dry mustard, Worcestershire sauce, garlic powder, pepper, and cayenne pepper. Reduce the heat to medium-low and simmer for 5 minutes.

- Meanwhile, fill a large pot with salted water and bring to a boil. Add the macaroni, stir, and cook for 2 minutes less than the time recommended on the packaging.

- As soon as the pasta is in the cooking water, remove the pan of béchamel sauce from the heat and gradually whisk in the Cheddar cheese and Gruyère (or Pecorino).

½ teaspoon cayenne
pepper, or to taste

1lb (450g) macaroni or
other small dried pasta
shape

3 cups (300g) grated sharp
Cheddar cheese

1 cup (100g) grated
Gruyère or 1 cup (60g)
grated Pecorino Romano

- Drain the macaroni in a colander and immediately stir it into the cheese sauce. Pour the mixture into the prepared baking dish. It should be quite runny. Sprinkle the breadcrumb/cheese topping evenly over the surface of the macaroni.

- Bake until the top is golden brown and the sauce is beginning to bubble up the sides of the dish, about 30 minutes. Allow to cool for 5 minutes. Serve hot.

Note: For a variation on the classic, stir 1 cup (250g) diced ham or sautéed lardons and 1 to 2 cups (250g to 500g) frozen peas into the macaroni before pouring it into the dish.

LUKE'S BAKED ZITI

SERVES 8

I first fell in love with baked ziti as a kid at summer camp, and then my younger son, Luke, started requesting it while he was watching *The Sopranos*. Baked ziti is a bit of a piggy pasta recipe, so instead of using plain ricotta, I make a spinach and ricotta filling. Ziti might be difficult to find; use rigatoni or paccheri instead. Swap the ziti for lasagne sheets, and you can make a spectacular lasagne (recipe follows).

1 lb (450g) ziti (or rigatoni, paccheri, or lasagna sheets* if making lasagna)

1 recipe Classic Tomato Sauce (p. 332) or Veal and Sausage Ragù (p. 97)

Spinach Ricotta Filling (recipe follows)

2 6½-oz (185g) balls fresh mozzarella, cut into ½-inch cubes

1 cup (60g) grated Parmesan cheese, divided

- Prepare a large pot of boiling salted water for the pasta, and have ready a 9 by 13 by 3-inch (23 by 33 by 8 cm) ceramic gratin dish. Preheat your oven to 350°F (180°C) and set a rack in the middle position.

- Boil your pasta for 2 minutes less than indicated on the package (it should be al dente). Scoop out a cup of the pasta water and set aside. Drain the pasta and place back in the pot.

- Cover the base of the gratin dish with a generous cup of the pasta sauce, then pour the remaining sauce into the pasta and stir until it is well coated. It should be quite wet and drippy at this point. If it isn't, stir in as much pasta water as needed to loosen it up.

- Spread one-third of the pasta over the base of the gratin dish, then spoon half of the ricotta mix every few inches over the surface in dollops, spacing them a few inches apart, along with one-third of the mozzarella cubes and ¼ cup of the Parmesan.

- Spread over another third of pasta and spoon the rest of the ricotta mix over the surface, then scatter over another third of the mozzarella cubes along with another ¼ cup of Parmesan. And, finally, spread over the last of the pasta and top with the remaining mozzarella cubes and last ½ cup of Parmesan.

- Cover the pan with aluminum foil and place in the oven for 30 minutes. Remove the pan from the oven, remove

the foil, and then bake for another 15 minutes, or until
the top is golden and bubbling. Let sit for at least 10
minutes to cool before serving.

For lasagna

- Prepare a large pot of boiling salted water for the pasta
  as well as a 9 by 13 by 3-inch (23 by 33 by 8 cm) ceramic
  gratin dish. Preheat your oven to 375°F (190°C) and set
  a rack in the middle position.

- Boil the lasagna sheets until al dente. Drain and rinse
  with cold water, then lay out individually on a clean
  kitchen towel.

- Spread a bit of tomato sauce (or the veal and sausage
  ragù) over the bottom of your dish and arrange a layer
  of lasagna sheets overtop. Spread over one-third of the
  sauce and dot the surface with a third of the mozzarella
  cubes and $1/4$ cup of the Parmesan. Arrange a second
  layer of lasagna noodles overtop and then spread over
  half the ricotta mix. Repeat these two steps again and
  finish with a final layer of pasta sheets and spread over
  the remaining sauce. You should have five layers of
  lasagna sheets in all. Top with the remaining mozzarella
  cubes and then sprinkle over the remaining $1/2$ cup
  Parmesan to cover the surface.

- Cover the pan with a lightly oiled sheet of aluminum foil
  and place the pan in the oven for 30 minutes. Remove
  the foil and then bake for another 15 minutes, or until
  the top is golden and bubbling. Let sit for at least 10
  minutes to cool before eating.

**Note:* I prefer traditional lasagna noodles to the no-boil
ones because they have a firmer texture and bake more
evenly.

SPINACH RICOTTA FILLING

MAKES ABOUT 3 CUPS (750g)

This recipe also works well for filling cannelloni,
or stuffing chicken breasts.

1 5oz (142g) container baby spinach OR 1 bunch (about 250g) large leaf spinach, washed (see p. 53)

2 cups (475g) fresh ricotta

1 small garlic clove, minced

1/2 cup (40g) grated mozzarella

1/2 cup (30g) grated Parmesan cheese

1 egg

1/4 cup (60ml) whipping cream

1 tablespoon chopped fresh basil

1/4 teaspoon nutmeg

1/2 teaspoon each salt and freshly ground pepper

1/2 teaspoon dried thyme

- Heat a large pot over medium-high heat and prepare an ice bath. Add a few spoonfuls of water to the hot pot, followed by the spinach all at once, and cover. After about 30 seconds, remove the lid and stir. Repeat the process until the leaves have just wilted, then transfer them to the ice water to cool. Remove the spinach from the water and squeeze it into a ball to remove as much liquid as possible. You can squeeze it further in a clean kitchen towel, then chop it into small pieces.

- In a medium bowl, combine the spinach with the ricotta and all the remaining ingredients. Mix well and use at once, or keep refrigerated until needed.

AN AMAZING SHEPHERD'S PIE

Known as Pâté Chinois in Quebec, Shepherd's Pie is a challenge to make sound
exciting because so many of us grew up eating it in that dullest of dining destinations:
the school cafeteria. And chances are that Shepherd's Pie wasn't even the real deal,
because an authentic Shepherd's Pie is made with ground lamb, whereas one made with
beef is known as Cottage Pie. And then there's Hachis Parmentier, the corn-free French
dish consisting of shredded pot roast topped with mashed potatoes. In restaurants,
I've enjoyed many variations on the theme, including versions made with duck,
deer, bison, and even foie gras. Everyone in my house loves Shepherd's Pie,
so I worked hard to make one I like. This version, I love.

1 tablespoon olive oil

2lbs (900g) best-quality
ground beef or lamb

Salt and freshly ground
pepper

1 medium onion,
chopped fine

White of 1 leek, rinsed
and chopped fine

2 carrots, peeled and
chopped fine

1 large garlic clove,
chopped fine

2 tablespoons tomato paste

2 tablespoons all-purpose
flour

1 cup (250ml) red wine

3 tablespoons (45ml)
Worcestershire sauce

3 cups (750ml) beef broth

A few branches fresh thyme

→

- Have ready a 9 by 13 by 3-inch (23 by 33 by 8 cm) gratin
  dish. Heat the oil in a large frying pan over high heat
  and add the meat, breaking it up into pieces. Stir well,
  season with salt and pepper, and sauté, breaking up
  any large chunks as you go, until the liquid evaporates
  and the meat begins to brown. Add the onion, leek, and
  carrot, reduce the heat to medium-high, and cook until
  the vegetables have softened, about 3 minutes. Add the
  garlic and sauté for a minute more.

- Stir in the tomato paste and Worchestershire sauce,
  and cook for another minute, then add the flour and
  continue stirring until it disappears. Pour in the wine,
  stir well, and let the mixture come to a boil. Let it
  bubble away until most of the wine boils off, then stir in
  the beef broth and thyme. Reduce the heat to medium
  and let simmer until most of the liquid is evaporated
  but the meat is still moist, about 10 minutes. Remove
  the thyme, pour into the gratin dish, spread out evenly,
  and set aside.

→

(continued)

Creamed Corn*

1 recipe Béchamel (p. 77)

2 tablespoons sugar

Freshly ground pepper
to taste

½ cup (30g) grated
Parmesan cheese

1lb (450g) frozen
corn kernels

- Once your béchamel is prepared, stir in the sugar and pepper. Let the mixture boil for a few seconds (keep stirring to prevent sticking), remove from the heat, and then whisk in the cheese. Add the corn, place back on the burner, and stir over medium heat to warm through without bringing it to a boil. Check the seasonings, adding more salt and pepper if needed, remove from the heat, cover, and set aside.

Mashed Potatoes

1½lbs (680g) Yukon Gold
or Russet potatoes

Salt

¾ cup (180ml) milk

¼ cup (60ml) whipping
cream

6 tablespoons (80g)
cold butter

½ teaspoon salt

Freshly ground pepper
to taste

- Peel the potatoes, cut into large cubes, and then place in a pot with enough cold water to cover by about 2 inches. Add 1 tablespoon of salt, bring to a boil, and cook until fork-tender, about 15 minutes. Meanwhile, in a small pot, heat the milk and cream together to a boil, and set aside.

- Drain the potatoes, place back in the pot, and mash thoroughly. Over medium heat, stir in the cold butter a couple of tablespoons at a time, then gradually blend in the hot milk. Season with the salt and pepper.

Assembly

2 tablespoons melted butter

3 tablespoons grated
Parmesan cheese or
1 teaspoon paprika

- Preheat your oven to 400°F (200°C). Spoon the creamed corn over the surface of the meat base in the gratin dish and spread into an even layer. Next, spoon over the mashed potatoes and spread into an even layer. Swirl the potatoes as you would frosting on a cake to create a wavy texture. You could also make ridges with the tines of a fork.

- Brush the melted butter over the potatoes. Scatter the cheese over the top, or simply sprinkle with paprika, which is more authentic.

- Bake for 40 minutes, or until the filling is bubbling around the edges and the top is a deep golden brown. Let rest for about 10 minutes before serving.

***Note:** The creamed corn recipe is time-consuming, so to cut corners, you could replace it with two 14oz (398ml) cans of creamed corn. But the homemade version is so delicious that I firmly believe it is time well spent.

THAI TURKEY MEATBALLS

SERVES 4

I love Thai cuisine and, when working as a restaurant critic, I always jumped
at the opportunity to review Thai restaurants. Sadly, Montreal is not exactly
Thai restaurant central, so I try to incorporate Thai flavors into family meals
whenever I can, and these meatballs are a perfect example. For a fun variation,
try making them with two-thirds ground pork and one-third chopped raw shrimp.

About ½ cup (70g) all-purpose flour for rolling

1 lb (450g) ground turkey or chicken

½ cup (55g) breadcrumbs

1 egg, lightly beaten

2 tablespoons milk

1 garlic clove, minced

1 tablespoon minced fresh ginger

1 tablespoon minced chili pepper

2 tablespoons chopped scallions

2 tablespoons chopped fresh cilantro

→

- Preheat the oven to 350°F (180°C). Prepare two baking sheets: Line one with parchment paper and sprinkle it with a thin layer of flour. Line the other with aluminum foil.

- In a large bowl, using your hands, combine all the ingredients except for the cooking oil and the sauce. Using 2 tablespoons or a 2-tablespoon (30 ml) ice cream scoop, portion out the mixture into approximately 30 mounds and place them on the floured baking sheet. With lightly floured hands, roll the mounds into rounds, then roll them in the flour to lightly coat.

- Heat a large frying pan over medium-high heat and add the cooking oil. When the oil is very hot, add the meatballs, about 10 at a time, and fry until golden brown on all sides. Place the fried meatballs on the foil-lined baking sheet while you continue frying all the rest. Place the meatballs in the oven and bake for 5 minutes or so, or until they are cooked through.

→

(continued)

1 tablespoon soy sauce

1 tablespoon Thai fish sauce

1/2 teaspoon salt

Generous pinch of sugar

3 tablespoons cooking oil
(ideally peanut oil)

Red curry sauce
(recipe follows)

Garnish:

1/2 cup cilantro leaves

1/2 cup coarsely
chopped scallions

1 lime, cut in half, one
half cut into 4 wedges

Rice (p. 251)

- Add the meatballs all at once into the bubbling sauce and stir gently to coat them well in the sauce.

- Transfer the meatballs to a large serving bowl and sprinkle over the cilantro and scallions. Squeeze over the juice of the 1/2 lime and serve with the lime wedges on the side, with a generous bowl of the rice.

Note: The meatballs can also be baked on the foil-lined pan under the broiler, turning frequently, until golden brown on all sides and cooked through.

Note: If you want to freeze the meatballs, simply freeze them on a parchment-lined baking sheet in one layer, then pile them in freezer bags. The meatballs can be left to defrost at room temperature for about 30 minutes, then floured and panfried; simply increase the cooking time by about 5 minutes.

Red Curry Sauce

2 tablespoons peanut
or canola oil

3 tablespoons Thai red
curry paste

2 tablespoons finely
chopped shallots

2 tablespoons finely
chopped fresh ginger

1 red chili pepper, finely
chopped

2 tablespoons finely
chopped garlic

1 14oz (400ml) can coconut
milk

About ½ cup fresh
basil leaves, ripped

2 tablespoons Thai
fish sauce

- In a large frying pan, heat the oil over high heat. Add the curry paste and fry in the oil, stirring in a circular motion, until the oil has absorbed the paste. Add the shallots, ginger, chili, and garlic and cook for about a minute. Pour in half the coconut milk, stir well, and then add the rest of the coconut milk. Bring to a boil and reduce the liquid by a third. Stir in the basil and fish sauce, cover, and cook for 1 minute.

Winter and Après-Ski

Montrealers love their outdoor sports. Besides the local religion known as hockey, there's skiing (either downhill or cross-country), snowboarding, skating, snowshoeing, tobogganing, dogsledding, walking to the top of Mont-Royal . . . you name it. It's our way of taking advantage of the snowy weather and getting outside in temperatures that demand you either move it or freeze on the spot.

Naturally, most winter activities merit a serious meal. After burning all those calories staying warm, you not only crave a feast, you've earned it! Or so I tell myself when ordering a large poutine at the ski chalet after the first run.

In Quebec, there are countless recipes for dishes intended for hunters, farmers, workers, maple syrup harvesters, and anyone relying on some serious carbohydrates to get through the day. In this chapter, I've got you covered!

There are some Québécois dishes that are simply too specialized for me to make at home. Cipaille, for instance, is a large pie made by layering an assortment of game meats and birds. Ragout de pattes consists of braised pig's feet, which I enjoy but cannot eat in vast quantities without feeling like I'll need a spa visit to recover. However, I'm a big fan of tourtière, or should I say meat pie (more on that later), and I will never turn down a bowl of cheese-topped, gravy-soaked homemade poutine. Never made poutine at home? Now's your chance!

I also like to go further down the cheese route with an elaborate raclette spread or, even better, a sumptuous fondue. Not just an après-ski classic, fondue is the ideal date-night dinner, as the opportunities for flirtatious forkplay are many.

Hot chocolate is another must when returning from outdoor activities. And when there's cocoa on the table, there had better be a plate of cookies. As for the ultimate cold-weather dessert? My pick would be another Québécois favorite, Pouding Chômeur (p. 283). Topped with a hot maple and cream sauce, this simple pudding cake is as beloved by French Canadians as Céline Dion and Denis Villeneuve. Our winters may be tedious, but they pass by quickly when you reward outdoor activities with treats like these.

AUTHENTIC SWISS FONDUE

SERVES 2

This recipe was shared by Raoul Colliard, a renowned fondue restaurateur I met at the Montreal High Lights Festival in 2015 who has been running the Buvette de Saletta wine bar in the Swiss Alps since 1985. "The secret is to use two-thirds Vacherin Fribourgeois extra, and one-third Gruyère," he explained. "No Emmental!" It's worth seeking out the Vacherin in cheese shops in your area, because Colliard's fondue is extraordinary. And don't forget, when you reach the bottom of the pot, whisk in an egg and scoop it up with the last of the bread. Yum!

1 garlic clove, peeled

½ tablespoon cornstarch

½ cup (125ml) dry white wine

1 ¼ cups (140g) grated Gruyère cheese

2 ¼ cups (260g) grated Vacherin Fribourgeois cheese

Freshly ground pepper

Baguette (or other crusty bread), cut into bite-size cubes

Kirsch (optional)

- Crush the garlic and rub it against the sides and bottom of your fondue pot. Place the pot on the stove over medium-high heat. Add the cornstarch and wine, whisk until smooth, and bring to a boil.

- Reduce the heat to low and sprinkle in the Gruyère, stirring continuously with a spatula until it melts. Add the Vacherin and melt over low heat. Add pepper to taste.

- As soon as the mixture reaches a creamy consistency, but before the first signs of boiling, transfer the pot to your fondue stand above the can of Sterno.

- Using a fondue fork, prick a piece of bread, dip it lightly in a little kirsch, if desired, plunge it into the pot, twirl to coat the bread in melted cheese, and then . . . devour! Stir the mixture every so often to prevent the fondue from sticking (or burning) on the bottom of the pot.

Note: Cheese fondue should be served in a heat-resistant pot that can be placed over a flame. It's best to use fondue sets with enamel or ceramic pots, which are available from kitchen stores.

PIZZA FONDUE

This is an ideal recipe for an après-ski family dinner, especially with kids who love pizza. It's also less expensive than classic fondue and it's easier to track down the cheeses required. To give the fondue an extra kick, I stir in a bit of grated Parmesan just before serving.

2 cups (225g) grated Emmental cheese

2 cups (225g) grated Gruyère cheese

2 tablespoons cornstarch

1½ cups (375ml) canned diced Italian tomatoes

1 garlic clove, peeled and minced

Salt, freshly ground pepper, and dried oregano to taste

½ cup (30g) grated Parmesan cheese

Suggested Accompaniments

2 loaves of Italian bread or focaccia, cut into 1-inch (2.5 cm) cubes

Assorted cut-up vegetables, such as peppers, mushrooms, and blanched broccoli and asparagus

Sliced pepperoni, cooked Italian sausage, cooked tortellini, OR cooked shrimp

- In a large bowl, toss the Emmental and Gruyère with the cornstarch. In your fondue pot, over medium-high heat, heat the diced tomatoes along with the minced garlic. When the tomato mixture begins to boil, begin adding the cheese mixture by the handful and stir with a wooden spoon in a figure-eight motion until the mixture is well combined, the cheeses have melted, and the fondue begins to bubble. Season with salt, pepper, and oregano to taste and stir in the grated Parmesan. Transfer the pot to your fondue stand above the can of Sterno.

- Serve with the accompaniments of your choice.

LET'S TALK TOURTIÈRE! OR
SHOULD I SAY, MEAT PIE?

If Julia Child was the woman who introduced French cooking to America, Je-hane Benoît was her equivalent in Quebec, and eventually throughout Canada. Mme Benoît's success preceded that of Mme Child and, like Child's, her books featured French recipes. However, a large part of her repertoire was devoted to traditional Québécois dishes, from ragout de pâtes to cretons to sugar pie. No doubt her most famous recipe was for tourtière.

I found her original tourtière recipe made with a mix of ground pork, onion, spices, and breadcrumbs. I then tried it out and . . . disaster! I don't know if it's because pork is so much leaner today than in 1963, when her recipe was published, but the resulting filling was dry, dull, and crumbly. After asking around for advice, I was told to add some mashed potato and even some of the potato cooking water to the mix. I did, and the results were excellent. I also upped the spices and ended up doubling the amount of filling to make a nice thick pie.

Authenticity sticklers would insist that the tourtière I'm describing is not a tourtière at all but a pâte à la viande (meat pie). Technically, tourtière and meat pie are both part of the family of dough-encased savory pies. But the difference is that the real-deal tourtière is filled with cubed meat, whereas a meat pie is made with ground meat. I've also read that an authentic tourtière must contain pork. I'm sure there are other theories as well.

So, the recipe below is indeed for a meat pie. I stand corrected—even though to me it will always be a tourtière, probably because I, like so many Montrealers, grew up eating La Belle Fermière tourtière, which was also a meat pie.

I'd never had much success making this Québécois classic, but after some tests, I think my take on Mme Benoît's tourtière is quite fabulous. Just be sure that your potato water isn't too salty and that your pie dough is at least partly made with lard. Mme Benoît was the spokesperson for the Canadian brand of lard called Tenderflake, so no doubt she would approve.

TOURTIÈRE (OKAY, OKAY . . . , MEAT PIE)

SERVES 6

Adapted from a recipe in Madame Jehane Benoît's *Encyclopédie de la cuisine canadienne.*

2lbs (1kg) ground pork

1 medium yellow onion, finely chopped

3 garlic cloves, minced

1 teaspoon salt

1 1/2 teaspoons dried savory

1 teaspoon celery powder (or salt)

1 teaspoon freshly ground pepper

1/2 teaspoon ground cloves

1 cup (250ml) water

About 2 to 4 tablespoons breadcrumbs

1/2lb (250g) potatoes, peeled

1 recipe Flaky Pie Dough made with lard (p. 329)

- Place the pork, onion, garlic, salt, herbs, spices, and water in a large saucepan and bring to a boil. Reduce the heat to medium-low and cook uncovered, stirring often, for about 20 minutes. Remove from the heat and stir in a few spoonfuls of breadcrumbs to absorb any excess fat.

- Meanwhile, boil the potatoes in 2 cups (500ml) of lightly salted water (be very careful about how much salt you add to the water, because you will use this water later on) until tender. Drain the potatoes, reserving 1 1/4 cups (300ml) of the cooking water. Mash the potatoes with the back of a fork and stir them into the meat mixture. Gradually stir in 1 cup of the potato water, mix well, and cook over medium-high heat for a few more minutes. Only add the rest of the water if the mix seems dry. You want a filling that is moist yet holds its shape. Remove from the heat and let cool completely.

- Roll out one round of dough to line a 9-inch (23 cm) pie plate with a few inches of overhang. Roll out the second round of pastry dough to the same size as the bottom round, then spoon the meat filling into the lined pie plate, being careful to keep the edges of the dough very clean. Brush the perimeter of the bottom crust lightly with water and then lay the second sheet of dough over the filling. Seal the two crusts together by lightly pressing on the rim, and then trim off any excess. Shape a decorative border if you like, and cut a small hole in the center of the top crust to allow the steam to escape while cooking.

- At this point, you can either refrigerate the tourtière until you are ready to bake it or bake right away.

- **To bake:** Preheat your oven to 400°F (200°C). Brush the top crust with the beaten egg and bake until golden brown, about 45 to 50 minutes. Eat hot or warm.

POUTINE

Whether from a ski hill canteen, late-night diner, roadside snack bar, or fancy restaurant, poutine—that decadent layering of French fries, gravy, and cheese curds—is one of Quebec's great comfort foods.

Local historians have traced poutine's origins to the late 1950s in the town of Warwick, between Quebec City and Montreal, and to the early '60s in the town of Drummondville (some 50 kilometers away), with different theories about how it was created in each. Debates persist, but what's clear is that the three key components (French fries, gravy, and fresh Cheddar cheese curds) have remained the same, and that poutine was not a Montreal invention, but a Québécois dish.

As a kid in the '70s, I recall seeing poutine at ski hill canteens, where it was sold alongside my preferred "frites sauce" (fries with gravy). In Montreal, the famous poutine restaurant La Banquise only added poutine to their menu in the '80s. But besides being an after-hours favorite (often touted as a hangover cure), poutine was never a dish you'd find in a fancy restaurant.

All that changed in 2001, when chef Martin Picard opened Au Pied de Cochon and wowed Montrealers with a half-dozen signature dishes like duck in a can and the foie gras–stuffed pig's foot. But it was his foie gras–topped poutine that caught everyone's attention and started a North American craze for poutine in high-end restaurants. It not only became the symbol of Picard's groundbreaking highbrow-meets-lowbrow style, but it also inspired several of Canada's top chefs to feature poutine on upscale menus with toppings like duck confit, braised lamb, or even lobster.

Long considered a bit of an embarrassing local dish by Quebecers (it's snack-bar food, after all), poutine rapidly garnered fans across Canada and the world. I've eaten poutine in Bermuda, Los Angeles, and Paris, and you'll find it everywhere from Hong Kong to Berlin.

Yet versions from outside Quebec tend to pale in comparison to the real deal. The sauce is often fancier than the authentic starch-thickened gravy. Some are topped with grated Swiss cheese or cubed mozzarella, lacking the correct flavor and that essential "squeak" when chewed—the hallmark of a fresh Cheddar-cheese curd.

In 2017, a survey by *Maclean's* magazine named poutine Canada's most iconic dish, and soon arguments broke out as to whether poutine, a Quebec signature dish if ever there was one, was being culturally appropriated across Canada. I tend to agree. Even if it's often disdained, poutine is a Quebec original that remains an important part of this province's culinary heritage. By labeling it "Canadian" we're not so much celebrating a true national dish as ignoring its regional origins.

Appropriation arguments aside, if you want to have a go at it at home, my version follows.

POUTINE

Poutine isn't usually a dish you make at home. First, you must have access to fresh cheese curds, and second, the sauce is a challenge to get right. I think this recipe comes pretty close to the classic. You can either make your fries from scratch or use commercial frozen fries, but I'd suggest frying them instead of oven-baking. As for the cheese topping, I find mine generous, but go crazy if you like.

Sauce

**MAKES ABOUT
2 CUPS (500ML)**

1 tablespoon extra-virgin olive oil

1 shallot, chopped

1 garlic clove, chopped

1 tablespoon maple syrup, plus more to taste

1 tablespoon cider vinegar

2 cups (500ml) reduced-sodium beef broth

1 tablespoon tomato paste

2 bay leaves

A few drops of Worcestershire sauce

Pinch of savory

1 1/2 tablespoons HP sauce (or other steak sauce)

1/2 teaspoon dry mustard

3 tablespoons cornstarch

1/3 cup (80ml) cold water

1 teaspoon salt

1/2 teaspoon freshly ground pepper

- In a saucepan over medium heat, heat the olive oil and brown the shallot and garlic. Add the maple syrup and stir to reduce for about 30 seconds, then deglaze with the vinegar. Add the broth, tomato paste, bay leaves, Worcestershire sauce, savory, HP sauce, and dry mustard. Bring to a boil.

- Dissolve the cornstarch in the cold water, stirring until smooth, and then whisk into the boiling sauce. Bring back to a boil, stir, and remove from the heat.

- Season with a few drops of maple syrup, the salt, and pepper. Remove the bay leaves and keep the sauce warm. Just before serving, whisk well and taste again to adjust the seasonings (poutine sauce should be on the salty side).

To assemble the poutine

1lb (500g) freshly fried French fries

1/2lb (250g) fresh cheese curds, or to your taste

- Fill a large serving bowl with half the fries. Add one-third of the cheese curds, pour over enough sauce to moisten, and then add the rest of the fries, followed by the remaining cheese curds. Pour over enough sauce to cover but not drown the fries (I don't use all the sauce, but you might want to) and serve immediately. A hot poutine waits for no one.

HOT CHOCOLATE

I made plenty of hot chocolate as a kid, always heavy on the sugar and cocoa powder.
When I was working as a pastry chef in France, we made it with chocolate instead
of cocoa, which gives it a silkier texture. This is the way I like it today, with just a
touch of cinnamon on top and, for special occasions, whipped cream.

1 1/2 cups (375ml) milk

1/4 cup (60ml)
whipping cream

2oz (56g) 70% chocolate

Cinnamon and/or sweetened
whipped cream to garnish
(optional)

- In a small pot, bring the milk and cream to a boil.
Meanwhile, chop the chocolate and place in a small
bowl. Pour one-third of the hot liquid over the
chocolate, wait half a minute, and then whisk until all
the chocolate is melted and the mix is glossy. Gradually
pour the rest of the hot liquid over the chocolate and
then, if it isn't hot enough to your liking, pour it back
into the pot and give it another blast of heat (I don't like
to bring it to a rolling boil, because hot chocolate takes
forever to cool). Pour into 2 cups and top each with a
pinch of cinnamon if you like, or, for a special occasion,
a spoonful of whipped cream. Why not both?

HAZELNUT AND CHOCOLATE CHIP COOKIES

MAKES 32 SMALL OR 16 LARGE COOKIES

I created this recipe for a famous brand of chocolate-hazelnut spread, and I adored the results. Serve these after the cheese course at your next dinner party with a bowl of clementines, and you have dessert. With a glass of port, they're even better!

1 1/4 cups (175g) all-purpose flour

1/4 teaspoon baking soda

1/4 teaspoon baking powder

1/4 teaspoon salt

1/2 cup (110g) unsalted butter

1/2 cup (100g) sugar

1/2 cup (100g) packed brown sugar

1/3 cup (100g) chocolate-hazelnut spread

1 egg

1 teaspoon vanilla

1/2 cup (50g) roughly chopped toasted and skinned hazelnuts

1/3 cup (75g) chocolate chips

- In a small bowl, whisk together the flour, baking powder, baking soda, and salt. Set aside.

- In the bowl of a stand mixer fitted with the paddle attachment, or in a bowl using a hand-held mixer, beat together the butter, sugars, and spread at high speed until creamy. Blend in the egg and vanilla and beat until very light and creamy, about 3 minutes. Blend in the dry ingredients on low speed, just until the flour disappears, then add the nuts and chocolate chips and mix just to combine. Do not overwork the dough.

- Using a 2-inch (5 cm) diameter ice cream scoop for small cookies or a 4-inch (10 cm) scoop for large cookies, portion out the dough into 32 small balls or 16 large onto a tray. You can also do this using two spoons. Refrigerate for 30 minutes.

- Preheat your oven to 350° F (180°C). Place the dough balls on two parchment-lined cookie sheets, leaving a few inches between them, and bake for 14 to 15 minutes, rotating the pans halfway through baking. They should just begin to color around the edges. Let cool on a rack before eating.

Note: These cookies are even more delicious when sandwiched together with spoonfuls of chocolate-hazelnut spread.

HANDS OFF MY COOKIES COOKIES

I have two sons who could live on cookies, so whenever I make a batch, they usually disappear before I can get my hands on even one. Then one day I put nuts in the cookies, and no one touched them. When I asked why, my 17-year-old fumed, "Why'd you have to go and put nuts in them?" Aha! Then I added pieces of candied orange peel to really drive them away. Score! But these cookies are so good that I'm afraid my kids will one day taste one and I'll have to think up a new ingredient to fend them off. I'm thinking anchovies . . .

½ teaspoon salt

½ teaspoon baking powder

½ teaspoon baking soda

½ cup (65g) pastry flour

1 cup (140g) all-purpose flour

⅛ teaspoon nutmeg

½ cup (110g) butter, at room temperature

⅓ cup (70g) packed brown sugar

½ cup (100g) sugar

¼ cup (40g) chopped candied orange peel OR the finely grated zest of 1 orange

1 egg

2 teaspoons vanilla

⅓ cup (35g) flaked sweetened coconut

- Prepare a baking sheet lined with parchment paper.

- Combine the salt, baking powder, baking soda, both flours, and the nutmeg in a bowl and whisk to combine. Set aside.

- In the bowl of a stand mixer fitted with the paddle attachment, or in a large bowl using a hand mixer, cream the butter with the two sugars until very light and fluffy, then beat in the orange peel (or zest). Blend in the egg and vanilla, scrape down the sides, and blend a bit more. Add the flour mix and blend on low speed just to combine, then add the coconut, chocolate, and nuts. Do not overmix.

- Using a ¼-cup measuring cup, portion out 12 equal-sized mounds of dough onto the prepared cookie sheet and roll each into a ball. Cover and refrigerate overnight.

- When ready to bake, preheat the oven to 350°F (180°C) and place an upside-down baking sheet in the oven on which you will place the cookie sheet (this prevents

⅓ cup (75g) chopped
semisweet chocolate OR
a mix of dark and milk
chocolate

1 cup (100g) best-quality
walnuts, roughly chopped

the cookies from overbaking on the bottom). Place the cookies on a parchment paper–lined cookie sheet (you can bake as many cookies as you like at a time and keep the rest of the dough refrigerated for up to a week) and bake for 20 minutes. Let cool completely before eating.

Note: If you don't have candied orange peel, you can use chopped dried cranberries or cherries, but the cookies won't have the same pizzazz as with the orange.

PART THREE

The word "apéro" has me conjuring up memories of meals in France where, upon arrival at someone's house, they'd pull out a half-dozen bottles of booze and ask me whether I'd like a Dubonnet or Pineau de Charentes. Following that, bowls of cherry tomatoes and olives would appear alongside boxes of cheesy snacks. It would carry on for a good hour while guests arrived, debates broke out, and someone passed around vacation pictures, and then, come dinner time, I'd be ready to have a nap on the couch.

It also reminds me of my mother's dinner parties in the '70s and '80s when, with pre-dinner cocktails, she'd come out with her famous party trio of bacon/liver roll-ups, crab dip, and meatballs drowned in a sweet-and-sour sauce. As odd as that sounds, they were delicious, and everyone hoovered up everything, which makes me wonder how they managed the multicourse meal she served afterwards.

That said, I love the French and Québécois tradition of the predinner drink-and-nibblies that is the apéro, but I've developed some rules to keep it short and sweet.

The quickest apéro I can recommend is a bottle of sparkling wine paired with a bowl of potato chips. The saltiness of chips works brilliantly with dry sparkling wine, and after a glass shared among friends, it's straight to the table. For a fancier affair, replace those chips with a bowl of everyone's favorite cheese puffs, known as gougères, and just watch them pounce.

If you prefer a drawn-out apéro, there are a few options. In summer, I like a bottle of rosé with a tray of tartines. In winter, I'll opt for a bottle of Beaujolais with a bowl of radishes, slices of saucisson sec (dry sausage), and a pot of mousse de foie de volaille (chicken liver pâté).

Just be sure not to overstuff your guests at the outset of the evening, to have a nonalcoholic drink planned (especially for the drivers), and to always have something to eat ready when you are serving alcohol, so people don't fall over.

Apéro!

GREEN GODDESS DIP

This classic American dressing was featured in my last book, and I love it so much that I turned it into a dip. It's brilliant with crudités, croutons, or pita chips.

½ cup basil leaves

¼ cup parsley leaves

¼ cup chervil or dill sprigs

2 tablespoons tarragon leaves

2 scallions, chopped

1 small garlic clove, minced

2 anchovy fillets, chopped

2 tablespoons lemon juice or white vinegar

¼ cup vegetable or olive oil

½ cup (110g) Greek yogurt

4oz (125g) cream cheese

½ teaspoon each of salt and freshly ground pepper, or more to taste

- In a blender, combine the herbs, scallions, garlic, anchovies, lemon juice (or vinegar), oil, yogurt, cream cheese, salt, and pepper. Blend at high speed until smooth. Scrape down the sides and blend again. Taste and adjust the seasonings to your liking.

- Serve immediately, or cover (with the plastic wrap pressed right against the surface) and store refrigerated for up to a day.

TAPENADE

This famous French condiment is ideal for pre-supper snacking, but it can also be
used to season meats or fish. This recipe comes from chef René Bérard of the
Hostellerie Bérard in the hilltop village La Cadière d'Azur in Provence.
Top-quality olive oil makes all the difference here.

1 generous cup (about
180g) black olives

6 anchovy fillets,
roughly chopped

1 generous teaspoon
chopped garlic

1 teaspoon capers

1 teaspoon finely grated
lemon zest

About 6 tablespoons
(90ml) extra-virgin olive oil

1 baguette (for the
croutons)

- Using the side of a wide knife, crush the olives to remove the pits, or use a cherry pitter. In a food processor, pulse-chop the olives, anchovy fillets, garlic, capers, and lemon zest until the mixture forms a paste.

- With the machine running, pour in enough olive oil to loosen the mix (it should fall easily from a spoon). Serve with croutons. Any leftover tapenade can be refrigerated, covered, for up to a month.

- To make the croutons: Preheat the oven to 400°F (200°C). Slice the baguette on a diagonal about $1/_2$-inch-thick (2 cm), place on a baking sheet, and toast until golden. Flip over and toast on the other side. Let cool.

Note on tartines: Much like Italian bruschetta, tartines consist of toasted or grilled bread spread with various toppings. At a cooking class I took in Avignon, the chef topped toasted sourdough with tapenade, goat cheese drizzled with honey, and roasted tomatoes (see p. 82) with fresh basil and a drizzle of olive oil. It's a casual start to dinner, but who wants to sit down for a plated appetizer when sipping rosé and nibbling tartines is much more fun?

SUN-DRIED TOMATO AND FETA DIP

MAKES 1 2/3 CUPS (430ML)

For this dip, I wanted to avoid rich ingredients like mayonnaise and sour cream, so
I used white beans for body, and sun-dried tomatoes and feta cheese for flavor.
This dip has a nice smoky taste that marries especially well with grilled shrimp.

1 14oz (398ml)
can cannellini beans,
drained and rinsed

1/2 cup (75g) sun-dried
tomatoes, roughly chopped

1/2 cup (about 90g)
cubed feta cheese

1/2 teaspoon salt,
or more to taste

1/4 teaspoon freshly ground
pepper, or more to taste

1 teaspoon hot sauce,
like Tabasco

1/2 teaspoon smoked
sweet paprika

1 garlic clove, peeled
and chopped

3 tablespoons extra-virgin
olive oil

1 teaspoon balsamic vinegar

1/2 cup (125ml) hot water

- Place the beans, sun-dried tomatoes, feta, salt, pepper, hot sauce, paprika, garlic, olive oil, and vinegar in a food processor. Pulse until smooth. With the motor running, gradually pour in the hot water. Purée until completely smooth and adjust the seasonings to taste.

- Serve with croutons and crudités or cooked shrimp. Store refrigerated for up to 3 days.

GOUGÈRES

These cheesy puffs may seem a little tricky, but even if they don't all look the same, they will taste great. Gougères pair brilliantly with sparkling wines and Champagne. I also love them cut in half and filled with chicken or tuna salad.

6 eggs

7 tablespoons (95g) unsalted butter, diced

1/2 teaspoon salt

1/2 cup (125ml) water

1/2 cup (125ml) milk

1 cup (140g) all-purpose flour

1 cup (100g) grated Gruyère or sharp Cheddar

1/4 teaspoon freshly ground pepper

1/4 teaspoon grated nutmeg

About 3 tablespoons grated Parmesan cheese for sprinkling

- Preheat the oven to 375°F (190°C) and line two baking sheets with parchment paper. Crack the eggs into a large measuring cup, whisk until smooth, and pour about 2 tablespoons into a small dish. Set aside.

- Combine the butter, salt, water, and milk in a saucepan and bring to a boil. Remove from the heat, add the flour all at once, and stir quickly with a wooden spoon until well blended. Return the pan to the burner over medium heat and keep stirring until the mixture forms a smooth ball that pulls away from the sides of the pan.

- Remove from the heat and let cool for a few minutes, then begin stirring in the whisked eggs a few spoonfuls at a time (you can do this by hand, or using a stand mixer with a paddle attachment on low speed).

- When the dough looks silky but not too firm or runny, stir in the grated Gruyère (or Cheddar) as well as the pepper and nutmeg.

- Using a piping bag fitted with a #4 (3/4-inch/1.5 cm wide) plain tip, pipe small mounds of batter, about the size of a walnut, onto the prepared sheets, leaving an inch of space between them. You can also use two teaspoons to form the balls. Don't worry about them being perfect, but try to keep them all the same size.

- Brush the mounds of dough with the reserved egg, and sprinkle with the Parmesan.

- Bake for 25 minutes, or until the gougères are puffed and golden (do not open the oven door during the first 10 minutes of baking). Turn off the oven, open the door just a crack, and leave the gougères in for another 5 minutes to prevent temperature shock, which might cause them to deflate. Transfer to a rack and let cool slightly before serving.

Note: You can make the gougères in advance and reheat before serving. Keep any leftovers in an airtight container at room temperature or in the freezer and reheat in a warm oven to restore their original texture.

JAMES MACGUIRE'S CHICKEN LIVER MOUSSE

SERVES ABOUT 10

I first tasted this divine mousse at the legendary Montreal restaurant Le Passe-Partout, whose chef-owner, James MacGuire, was renowned for many dishes, this being one of them. Despite a few adaptations, MacGuire humbly gives credit for this mousse to his mentor, the famous French chef Charles Barrier. Impressive credentials aside, this drop-dead-delicious mousse is easy to make, but be sure to follow the instructions to a T.

1 cup (250ml) whipping cream

1/2 cup (110g) unsalted butter, cut into pieces, at room temperature

1/2 cup (110g) rendered duck fat, at room temperature

1/2 lb (225g) duck or chicken livers (trimmed of nervy bits before weighing)

3 egg yolks

1 1/2 tablespoons Cognac or Armagnac

1 3/4 teaspoons salt

1/4 teaspoon freshly ground white pepper

A note about molds: Choose a 2 to 2 1/2-cup (500 to 625ml) ceramic terrine mold that's 3 to 4 inches (8 to 10 cm) deep, of any shape you like. The mixture will be about 2 inches (5 cm) deep, and the sides will rise a bit as it bakes. If you don't intend to serve it all at once, you can use several smaller molds. I usually make this in a small terrine mold and two ramekins of various sizes but all about the same depth.

- Preheat the oven to 325°F (160°C). Set out a baking pan large enough to hold the molds, place a thin kitchen towel at the bottom, and put on a full kettle of water to boil.

- Bring the cream to a boil and keep it hot. Blend the butter and duck fat in a food processor. Then, with the machine running, add the livers one or two at a time, followed by the egg yolks, one at a time. Stop and scrape down the sides of the bowl with a spatula. With the machine again running, and taking care not to splatter and burn yourself, gradually pour in the hot cream, followed by the Cognac (or Armagnac), salt, and pepper.

- Strain the mixture into a large measuring cup. Pour it into the mold (or molds), place it (or them) in the baking pan, and pour in enough boiling water to come up to the same level as the mousse mixture inside. Place a sheet of aluminum foil over the pan and wrap the edges around the rim to seal. Carefully place it into the oven and bake for 25 to 30 minutes, or until the internal temperature reads 165°F (74°C). The top of the mixture should be convex but without cracks, and the center of the mousse should be set. (Beware: If the mousse is baked too long, the small amount of air in it will cause it to rise like a soufflé, with disastrous results.)

- Carefully remove the pan from the oven, then lift the mold (or molds) out of the hot water. Immediately cover with plastic wrap, pressing it lightly against the surface of the mousse to keep it from oxidizing. Cool on a rack, then refrigerate to chill completely before serving. The mousse will keep for up to 4 days.

- **To serve:** Scrape off and discard the mottled surface from the top of the mousse and, with a tablespoon dipped in very hot water, form it into quenelle-shaped portions. Serve immediately.

Note: As an accompaniment, MacGuire suggests pickles and pain au levain. I like croutons or toast points made from Daily Bread (p. 20). As for wine, he prefers a Chenin moelleux from the Loire, while I quite like this with a lightly chilled Beaujolais.

APÉRITIF CAKE WITH HAM, CHEESE, AND OLIVES

SERVES 8

This savory "cake" is easy to make, takes just an hour to prepare, and is sure to please all your guests. This recipe is adapted from Sophie Dudemaine's classic book *Les Cakes de Sophie* (Minerva, 2001).

1 generous cup (150g) all-purpose flour

2 teaspoons baking powder

A good pinch each of salt and freshly ground pepper

3 eggs

1/3 cup (80ml) vegetable oil

1/2 cup (125ml) hot milk

1/2 cup (75g) green olives, pitted

1/2 cup (75g) finely diced ham

3/4 cup (75g) grated Gruyère cheese

- Preheat the oven to 350°F (180°C). Butter a 8½ by 4½ by 2½-inch (21 by 11 by 6 cm) loaf pan and line the base with parchment paper.

- Mix the flour, baking powder, salt, and pepper.

- In a medium bowl, beat the eggs with the dry ingredients to make a thick batter. Gradually blend in the oil, then add the hot milk a little at a time, mixing well.

- Fold in the olives and ham. Set aside a good pinch of the grated cheese and fold the rest into the batter. Pour the batter into the loaf pan, sprinkle with the reserved cheese, and bake for 50 minutes, or until golden brown on top. Cool completely on a wire rack, unmold, and slice.

ENTERTAINING
MONTREAL STYLE

How do Montrealers throw a dinner party? Well, I haven't thrown a dinner party in many other cities, but I can tell you how we do it around here. Or at least how this Montrealer does it. Dinner parties are great, unless you're the person throwing one. Then the pressure to produce the perfect evening can be overwhelming. I can roast a chicken, I can clean house, I can pick wines, I can carry a conversation at the dinner table, and I can even whip up a croquembouche in my sleep. Pulling all those elements together for a 4-hour dinner party, though? Not so easy. The last time I had people over for Thanksgiving, I answered the door in a dirty apron and house slippers. The turkey was fabulous, and the bathroom was spotless, yet somewhere along the way I had forgotten to clean up something even more important—me!

Why is it that some people can entertain with ease while others fall apart faster than a wedding cake in the back of a pickup truck? I grew up watching my mother give terrific dinner parties with silverware, china, a salad course, and a soufflé for dessert. But today we're encouraged to play it casual and invite our friends into the kitchen to stir the risotto. Ultimately, dinner parties either work or not due to one factor, and it's not good company, because good company turns to bad company if the food is lousy. Of course, it's the food. Even a mind-blowing Bordeaux can't make up for stringy steak.

Throwing a dinner party is no small feat. Ingredients are expensive, planning and cooking take time (something few of us have), and the thought of washing a mountain of pots at midnight is enough to scare most people away from even contemplating having the neighbors over for stuffed mushroom caps and lasagna. Yet despite the stress, a dinner party isn't just good fun but an important social custom. I'm all for restaurants, but a night of hospitality in someone's home is a truly heartwarming experience. The secret to making it work is not letting stress get the best of you, or, as the saying goes, never let them see you sweat—even if you forgot to shower.

TIPS FOR MAKING YOUR DINNER PARTIES A HIT

Let's be real, it's just a dinner party, so have fun with it. Here are some suggestions for making it work.

At my house, the best dinner parties are for 4 to 8 guests. Anything above that is hard to manage alone. Try to make sure that at least one guest is a close friend (better yet, a couple), someone you know well enough to ask midparty to clear a few dishes, to accept the burnt lamb shank, or to change that toilet paper roll upstairs that you completely forgot about.

In Montreal, dinner parties tend to be casual. Going out for dinner is a time for the big dressup, but when people come to my house for supper, I prefer to see them walking around in slippers rather than stilettos. And casual dressing makes everyone feel at home.

A seating plan is essential. Couples shouldn't be seated side by side, unless they insist, which is fine but a good reason not to invite them over again.

I always keep the menu simple. Three courses are plenty, but if you want to prolong the evening, add a cheese course. I know a lot of people offer a cheese platter (with pâté!) predinner, but in Montreal, cheese is always served after the main course. And on that note, be careful not to load everyone up with nibblies and stiff cocktails before the meal.

Make dishes you've already mastered. Now's not the time to try the cheffy dish from your favorite restaurant cookbook. And for the main course, avoid plating the food like they do in a restaurant. I far prefer large platters, which allow guests the option of taking as much (or as little) as they like.

If anyone offers to bring something, accept! Cheese and dessert are the best courses to farm out to friends.

When cooking, before even peeling a carrot, begin by cleaning up the kitchen as best you can. Rid your counters of any excess clutter. Wash down all surfaces. Scrub the sink clean. Tell anyone who isn't helping to scram. The sight of dishes piling up in the sink is always depressing, so fill the sink with hot soapy water in advance to facilitate the clean-as-you-go technique. And always start the night off with an empty dishwasher.

There's nothing wrong with store-bought anything. I always put out a bowl of chips and another one of olives. And rest assured that no one will know that the hummus and crudités with dip are store-bought when they're served on your fanciest plates.

Ideally, during the dinner party, you should be assembling and finishing off dishes instead of doing any time-consuming cooking, so try to prepare as much as possible in advance: peel and blanch vegetables (wrap in paper towels and hold in the fridge), wash your salad greens, make the vinaigrette and dessert.

Regarding booze: Here in Montreal, wine rules and beer isn't really dinner party fare. A cocktail or a bottle of bubbly to offer friends upon arrival is the preferred way to get the party started. Always have a bottle of red wine on hand even if your meal is better suited to white, because many people just prefer red. Serve your wines at the right temperature. Red wines should be served slightly below room temperature, at about 65°F (18°C) and white wine should be served at about 50°F (10°C), slightly above fridge temperature (unless they're cheap wines, then chill them hard). If guests bring wine, unless there's a penguin or kangaroo on the label, make it part of the meal and open it. If they brought it, they would probably like to taste it. Serve plenty of water along with the booze, and remember not to let friends get into a car inebriated. And don't forget the nonalcoholic beer or wine for those who choose not to drink.

When it comes to yourself, lay out your planned outfit first thing in the morning, wash your hair, and set aside a clean apron for the time you will be cooking when company is there. That goes for the guys too.

The day of the party, stop cooking an hour before your guests arrive, clean up the kitchen again, and then walk away. Take out the dog, read, treat yourself to a long bath, meditate, get ready. Only get back in there about 10 minutes before the guests are due to arrive.

The more you entertain, the less stressed out you'll be before a dinner party, because chances are you've either been trying too hard or you need practice. Inviting people over can be expensive and can rob you of a day, timewise, but it's a great way to bond with friends old or new. And let's face it, that extra hit of stress gave you a push to make everything great—or at least better than the usual family supper.

And finally . . . Clean your house thoroughly before a dinner party. Make the beds, clean the bathrooms. Change the hand towels, put away the toothbrushes, change that dirty water glass. Remove anything from the medicine cabinet that is too personal: the antidepressants, fungal creams, and Viagra give away too many secrets. Never assume friends don't snoop. They do.

AS FOR DÉCOR . . .

Don't feel the need to repaint the house or rush out and rent paintings from your local museum. On the flip side, however, don't neglect the small stuff, particularly the table setting. You made a great dinner, now give it a backdrop worthy of all that effort. Here are some suggestions:

Are place cards too *Downton Abbey*? No way! For a dinner of 6 or more guests, place cards set in front of each plate can help get people seated quickly. They also help if you can't remember your own seating plan (it happens). As for the seating arrangements, always seat the most entertaining guests in the middle seats to keep the conversation flowing.

Tablecloth versus placemats? I'm a fan of the tablecloth, a simple cotton or linen one, preferably white or a pale color. You don't have to spend a fortune on one; I've found pretty tablecloths at Ikea. To add a hit of color, try to mix-and-match the napkins and the tablecloth. As for napkins, use cloth, NEVER paper. I've had the same pile of multicolored linen napkins for 20 years, and they still look great.

Concerning wineglasses. For a casual supper, you can serve wine in any glass you want, but for a party, proper wineglasses are de rigeur. Why? Simply because a glass with a stem and thin lip will make your wine taste better. You can splurge on Riedel or Spiegelau glasses (which are often on sale in department stores), but today many less expensive brands sell excellent glasses too. And, if you start with white wine and then switch to red, you don't need to bother with a different glass for every course.

Candles? Yes! As many as your table can handle without it looking like a religious ceremony or seance. Also, dim the lights, but within reason. Candlelight gives off the most beautiful aura, but candlelight alone makes me feel like there's been a power failure. And avoid scented candles at all costs. It's a dinner party, not a spa session.

What about flowers? A flower arrangement will always get a big thumbs-up from me, but keep it small and low so that you can fit all the food on the table and see the person across from you when you speak instead of peering through a blur of peonies. Also, avoid any flowers with a strong smell. As much as I love lilies, they smell like a funeral home.

Concerning music. I like a bit of background music at a dinner party, but this is not the time to blare your favorite dance tunes or opera overtures. A bit of soft jazz, tango music, classical . . . Maybe I'm dating myself with those choices, but I'll take Sinatra over Miley Cyrus at a dinner party any day. An ad-free radio station can be a good choice too. But whatever you do, keep the volume low.

And if you're the guest . . . Arrive either on time or up to 15 minutes late. Don't assume you can wear shoes in the house (you can bring some slippers if need be). Arrive with a gift, such as a bottle of wine or olive oil, flowers, or something homemade (jam, cookies, the orange cake on p. 316). Try not to interrupt or hog the conversation at the table, and avoid topics that could cause tension. Help out if the host or hostess looks stressed. Don't drink too much and don't overstay your welcome. As soon as you see more than one person yawning at the table, it's time to call it a night. And don't forget to send a thank-you email note the next morning.

And always return the favor! If you had a great night at a friend's house, next time, you do the inviting.

MY WORST
DINNER PARTIES

I have thrown some excellent dinner parties in my time, but also many duds. Of those failures, I can think of two I would not want to relive again. Coincidentally, both were dinner parties for visiting winemakers.

The first was held in early fall for a winemaker from France. To honor his country and his wines, I prepared a traditional dish from his region for the appetizer. For the main course, I decided on an Asian-style duck dish served in a star anise and ginger broth. A selection of local cheeses would follow, with a simple pear tart for dessert to pair with one of his sweet wines. I invited 4 other guests, including a restaurateur and a fellow restaurant critic. Everything seemed well planned and, well . . . perfect.

The day of the party, the temperature hit an unseasonal 93°F (34°C). Watching my pie dough sticking to the counter, I felt that somehow this dinner was doomed. The other guests arrived on time, but the winemaker showed up quite late, no excuse or apology given.

When we got to the table, I noticed it was a bit cramped for 8 diners, with the wife of the restaurateur squashed into a corner beside the curtains. I had met the winemaker in France and found him pleasant. But that night, sitting at the head of my table, he couldn't have been more pompous.

When the first course arrived, he turned to me and asked why I had chosen that dish, saying it was completely ill-suited to his wines. What the . . . ? I shrank in my seat. When the second dish arrived, my now profusely sweating guests looked down at the steaming duck dish in despair, then sipped it unenthusiastically. By then, no one else at the table was speaking anymore, as the guest of honor had hijacked the evening, talking about himself and his wines ad nauseam.

By the time dessert came out, everyone was requesting a tiny piece, eager, no doubt, to get away from that table. Of course, the last person to leave that night was the winemaker, who regaled us with stories about himself until well after midnight.

The moral of the story: it only takes one bad guest to ruin a dinner party.

The second party was not for just one winemaker, but three. A fan of their wines, I doubled my usual effort to make a dinner to show off their bottles. My menu consisted of a wedge salad with blue cheese dressing, braised lamb shanks, and the famous Québécois maple pudding cake, pouding chômeur. The lamb was an expensive choice, but I figured that with a cheap appetizer and dessert, things would even out.

Of course, they all arrived late, and directly from the airport, so they were already tired. To my surprise, they weren't in the least bit interested in drinking their wines, so they opened others they had brought, sadly ill-suited to my menu. Okay . . .

To my relief, the wedge salad was a hit, though they looked at it for a few minutes puzzled that anyone would serve a thick triangle of iceberg lettuce as a starter, no matter what the dressing. The lamb shanks, however, were a total miss. I ordered the meat from a reputable butcher who presented me with a big bag of frozen shanks on arrival, apologizing that he didn't have fresh. I bought them but when they defrosted, it turned out these were the biggest lamb shanks (mutton shanks?) I had ever seen. Ugh.

I used a fiddly recipe that called for each shank to be wrapped in parchment paper with sauce. It's usually terrific, but that night . . . that night it was dull, and the portions were ridiculously large. The winemakers picked at it, leaving most of it on their plates. I was tempted to get into my car and drive to Vermont.

But then came the pouding chômeur, a delicious dessert I hoped would save the day. Not a chance. Instead of making one large portion, I had decided on individual portions, which I pulled out of the oven once they were bubbling and golden brown. Yes! As great as they looked, they were undercooked and pasty inside. The winemakers were as perplexed by my dessert as my starter. I should have just made steak frites and a big crème caramel and called it a day.

The moral of that story: sometimes when you try too hard to impress, you end up doing quite the opposite.

WHY I HATE POTLUCK SUPPERS (AND HOW TO MAKE THEM WORK)

When listing my worst dinner party experiences, I could easily have added almost every potluck meal I've held or attended. The one that stands out the most was a New Year's Eve potluck that began with a friend's black bean soup, which was so good that we all had 2 servings. After that came a rich French chicken dish. I then recall a cheese platter where every cheese was smellier than the last. And finally, a tarte Tatin that no one was interested in after all that heavy food.

The problem with a potluck is it's hard to control what's going to hit the table, and that's a challenge for those of us who like to plan a dinner right down to the angle of the sliced bread. And, let's be honest, some people are good cooks, others are not, so there's that fear that comes with the unknown.

But people like to chip in, and a potluck is also a great way to cut costs. So here are some tips for making it work.

Choose a team leader: One person should oversee who brings what, or you risk having 5 desserts and a dip.

Set a theme: Settle on a style of cuisine, like French, Italian, or barbecue; otherwise, get ready for a meal of spring rolls, coq au vin, and tiramisu. No thanks.

Timing is key: Insist everyone shows up on time to get all the dishes sorted, as well as refrigerated or reheated if necessary. I once attended a potluck where the person bringing the main course showed up an hour late. Not good.

When in doubt, go green: If your meal is already planned and a last-minute guest insists on bringing a dish, make it salad, because a salad will always get eaten.

About the friends who can't cook: Ask them to bring cheese, suggesting even which ones to bring and—why not?—a good cheese shop in their area.

The main event: The person who is holding the potluck should be the one in charge of the main course because it's probably going to be hot and the most difficult to transport.

What about the vino? When it comes to wine, give that responsibility to the friend who knows the difference between Pinot Noir and Chardonnay, who won't bring a lousy bottle, and who will enjoy the task. As wine is pricey, this responsibility can be farmed out to a few friends if you require several bottles.

Find the baker: As for dessert, ask the friend who loves to bake instead of the one who'll show up with a supermarket mousse cake picked up on the way to the party.

Talk it through: Be sure you discuss with the group likes and dislikes, as well as dietary restrictions and allergies. A chicken and sausage gumbo makes for a great potluck dish unless you're a vegetarian.

Don't phone it in: I once attended a potluck dinner where everyone brought beautiful food and wine and one guest showed up with a rutabaga. Let's just say, I haven't seen him since.

THREE MONTREAL COCKTAILS

Beauty and the Beet
FOR 1 COCKTAIL

This cocktail, created by Montreal mixologist Claudia Doyon, includes three common Québécois ingredients: pickled beet juice, maple syrup, and . . . gin!

1oz (30ml) gin, floral or pine-forward style

½oz (1 tablespoon/15ml) pickled beet juice

½oz (1 tablespoon/15ml) maple syrup

Ice cubes

3oz (90ml) dry sparkling wine

For this cocktail, you'll need to chill your glass, ideally a Champagne or coupe glass, in the freezer for a few minutes beforehand.

Combine all the ingredients except the sparkling wine in a shaker. Add ice and shake for about 6 to 8 seconds. Remove the remaining ice by straining the mixture into the glass. Top off with the sparkling wine. Stir gently with a spoon to blend.

Moishes Spritz
MAKES 1 COCKTAIL

Created by mixologist Olivier Bergeron, this is the
wildly popular signature spritz of Moishes restaurant
in Montreal.

1oz (30ml) Amermelade apéritif or Aperol

½oz (1 tablespoon/15ml) gin

½oz (1 tablespoon/15ml) St-Germain liqueur

½oz (1 tablespoon/15ml) Lillet blanc

2oz (60ml) Prosecco

Club soda

Ice cubes

Slice of orange and an olive to garnish

Fill a large wineglass with ice and add the first five
ingredients. Top off with club soda. Spear the orange
and olive and lay them on top of the glass.

Grilled-Strawberry Boulevardier
FOR 1 COCKTAIL

Sabrina Touzel, from the restaurant Foxy, created this take on the classic Boulevardier using local Quebec strawberries.

1½oz (45ml) Grilled-strawberry–infused bourbon (recipe follows)

1oz (30ml) Campari

1oz (30ml) sweet vermouth

1 strip orange peel

Grilled strawberry

Stir the bourbon, Campari, and vermouth together in a mixing glass filled with ice and strain into a rocks glass over a single large ice cube.

Squeeze the orange peel gently over the cocktail to express the oils, then discard the peel. Garnish with the grilled strawberry.

Grilled-Strawberry–Infused Bourbon
FOR 1 COCKTAIL

½ cup (about 75g) strawberries

12oz (1½ cups/375ml) bourbon, preferably Buffalo Trace

Grill the strawberries on your outdoor grill or in a grill pan until they are slightly black.

Place the grilled strawberries and bourbon in a container and let infuse for at least 24 hours; 48 hours is best.

Strain through a coffee filter, and it's ready to go.

4 SAMPLE MENUS

The Romantic Menu
Tartines with James MacGuire's Chicken Liver Mousse
Lobster Risotto
Caramel Ice Cream
Hazelnut and Chocolate Chip Cookies

The Mother's Day Brunch
Rhubarb Streusel Coffee Cake
Gravlax with Caraway and Coriander
Pink Salad
Asparagus and Ricotta Tart
Tomato Galette
Boston Cream Pie

The Impress-the-Foodie-Friends Dinner
Gougères
My Lipp Salad
Striped Bass with Roasted Fennel
and Tomatoes en Papillote
Cherry and Berry Clafoutis
Financiers

The Summer Celebration on the Terrace
Apéritif Cake with Ham, Cheese, and Olives
Tapenade and Croutons
Max's Mac 'n' Cheese (for children)
Now That's a Salade Niçoise! (for adults)
Berry Pavlova
Maple Pecan Pie

PART FOUR

FANCIER FARE

Home cooking can fall into myriad categories: breakfast, lunch, and dinner . . . Italian, Japanese, or French . . . sweet or savory. Dishes can also be classified by season, the wintry cheese fondue, the summery salads. But for home cooks, especially those who like to entertain, there are two more categories: everyday food and special-occasion food.

Of course, some people eat fancy food daily while others eat plain food on special occasions. Nothing wrong with that. However, I'm not one to serve an expensive roast beef for a family dinner, and spaghetti is not my first choice for a special occasion.

Much of the differentiation between casual and fine dining is based on cost, and price is certainly an issue when food shopping. But even if fancy dishes cost a bit more and take more time, they will always be less expensive than at a restaurant. As much as I love a night out, a dinner party at home will always be my preference.

That said, having worked as a restaurant critic for 20 years, the hundreds of Montreal eating establishments I have frequented have greatly influenced my home cooking. And I say "influenced," because I'm not a fan of overly cheffy recipes, preferring those that won't make me a prisoner in my own kitchen. So, I offer a few shortcuts for you to enjoy the meal along with your guests.

Fish can be tricky for dinner parties. It's pricey, it's not everyone's favorite, and it calls for precise cooking that requires one's full attention. But its advantages outweigh the disadvantages, because fish is a light and healthy choice, which suits many these days. When prepared simply, it's a quick cook. And fish is just so moist, delicate, and gorgeous that I've come to favor it for a special occasion. Just inquire first before assuming it's everyone's cup of tea.

As for meat, my approach has changed over the years. There was a time that the meat/starch/vegetable trio was the only way to go. Today the vegetable dish can play the leading role, with the meat and starch as accompaniments. I serve half the amount of meat you'd get in a restaurant, and often plate it in slices to give the impression of a larger portion.

Chicken has never been considered a luxury dish in restaurants, but at home I serve it at least once a week, as it remains one of the most affordable meats available. I hate food waste, so I always ask guests whether they like meats like duck or lamb before planning a menu. And if there are leftovers, never forget that cold shredded meat works beautifully incorporated into a pasta sauce the next day.

Fish and Seafood

SALMON TARTARE

SERVES 6 TO 8 AS CANAPÉS OR 2 AS AN APPETIZER

In my years as a restaurant reviewer, I tasted my share of both salmon and tuna tartare. The best were light on the onion and mayonnaise and included something to give them a little punch and crunch. I'm leaving the amount of hot sauce up to you, and for the crunch, I serve this with top-quality potato or vegetable chips.

½lb (225g) sushi-grade salmon fillet

2 to 3 tablespoons Antonio Sauce (recipe follows)

2 tablespoons finely chopped chives or scallions

2 tablespoons finely chopped red onion or shallot

½ teaspoon finely grated lemon zest

Hot sauce or Tabasco to taste

Salt and freshly ground pepper

Fresh lemon juice (optional)

Lettuce leaves and chips to serve

- Place your mixing bowl in the fridge to chill before beginning the recipe.

- Remove the skin from the salmon and cut the flesh into thin slices, removing all traces of blood or excess fat. Then cut the slices in the opposite direction, and then slice again in the first direction to make cubes. Chop again if you prefer a finer tartare texture.

- Place the salmon in your mixing bowl, add 2 tablespoons of the Antonio Sauce, the chives (or scallions), onion (or shallot), zest, a few dashes of hot sauce, a good pinch of salt, and a little pepper, and mix gently to avoid crushing the salmon flesh. Taste and add a dash of fresh lemon juice if you like, and more salt and/or hot sauce if necessary. You can also add the last spoonful of Antonio Sauce if you want a richer tartare. Taste one last time, and serve immediately, on a few lettuce leaves if you like with some vegetable chips or potato chips on the side.

ANTONIO SAUCE

MAKES 1 1/4 CUPS (375ML)

This recipe was graciously shared by chef Antonio Park of the Montreal restaurant Park. Any leftovers can be used as a dip or dressing for salads or grilled vegetables.

1/4 cup (20g) grated carrot

2 tablespoons chopped onion

1/4 cup (30g) grated green apple

1 tablespoon soy sauce

1 tablespoon maple syrup

1 tablespoon mayonnaise

1/4 cup (60ml) olive oil

- Combine all the ingredients except the mayonnaise and oil in a blender and blend to liquefy. Add the mayonnaise and blend a few seconds longer. With the machine running, drizzle in the oil to emulsify the sauce. Store any leftovers in the fridge, with plastic wrap pressed against the surface of the sauce.

STRIPED BASS WITH ROASTED FENNEL AND TOMATOES EN PAPILLOTE

I am a big fan of cooking en papillote, because everything can be assembled in advance and baked at the last minute. This recipe can also be made with black bass, red snapper, halibut, or cod. The first time I made it, I used wild striped bass from New Brunswick, and I have yet to taste a better fish dish.

1 large fennel bulb

1/2 cup (125ml) olive oil

Salt and freshly ground pepper

20 cherry tomatoes, sliced in half

1/4 teaspoon thyme leaves

4 Yukon Gold potatoes, about 3oz (85g) each, peeled

1 lemon, cut in half

1 medium shallot, peeled and minced

2 teaspoons capers, roughly chopped

1/4 cup torn basil leaves (or parsley or dill)

4 6oz (180g) striped bass fillets, preferably wild, skin on or off

- Preheat the oven to 375°F (190°C). Cut the fennel bulb lengthwise in half and then cut each half into 3 wedges. Do not remove the core, as this will hold the sections together. Rub the fennel with a tablespoon of oil and then sprinkle with salt and pepper. Place it in a small roasting dish, cover tightly with foil, and bake for 1 hour, or until you can easily pierce the sections with a sharp knife. Remove from the oven and let cool.

- Meanwhile, arrange the cherry tomatoes on a small parchment-lined baking sheet, cut side up, sprinkle with salt, pepper, and the thyme leaves, and place in the oven for the last half hour with the fennel while it bakes. Remove from the oven and let cool. Increase the oven temperature to 500°F (250°C).

- Place the potatoes in a pot of cold salted water and bring to a boil. When they are cooked through, drain and slice into 1/2-inch (1 cm) rounds. Set aside.

- Once the roasted tomatoes have cooled, place them in a small bowl and stir in the juice of one lemon half, the minced shallot, capers, remaining olive oil, and the basil leaves. Set aside. ·Cut the roasted fennel sections in half and slice the remaining lemon half into thin rounds.

→

(continued)

- Have at the ready a large baking sheet. Lay 4 large rectangles of parchment paper about 12 by 15-inches (30 by 38 cm) in size on your counter and arrange an equal amount of potato slices in the center of each sheet. Divide the fennel pieces equally among the 4 portions and then spoon 2 tablespoons of the tomato sauce over each. Next, season the fish fillets on the flesh side with salt and pepper and then place a fillet, skin-side up, over each portion of sauce and top with a round of lemon.

- Fold the top left-hand corner of each sheet of parchment over to meet the bottom right-hand corner and, starting at the left, tightly crimp the edges of the paper from left to right to seal the packages, forming half-moons and tucking under the final crimp. Place them in one layer on the baking sheet. The packages can be assembled and refrigerated several hours in advance. Just let them come to room temperature for 20 minutes before baking.

- Bake for 11 minutes for thin fish fillets, and 12 for thicker fillets, then immediately slide one package right onto each guest's plate, instructing everyone to rip open the packages (if they sit too long, the fish will keep cooking). Serve with any remaining tomato sauce alongside.

BAKED SALMON, TWO WAYS

I love so much about salmon, an emblematic fish of both Canada and Quebec. First, that it's readily available, though unless you have access to wild salmon, chances are that, like me, you are purchasing farmed fish. That said, I will go out of my way for organic farmed salmon (with the price that follows). Second, its versatility, as it pairs brilliantly with a multitude of flavors. And third, its quick cooking time, which, when properly gauged, results in that ideal silken/moist texture. As we all know, overcook your salmon by just a few minutes, and you might as well feed it to the cat. So, my advice is to err on the undercooked side, where you can easily pop it back in the oven for a minute or two.

Cooking a whole side of salmon is a great option for a dinner party, because you can have the hot fish on the table in 15 minutes and make the sauce in advance.

To roast a side of salmon

My idea here is to cook a side of salmon for 4 to 6. Keep the skin on, and for 4, request that the tail end be removed. I always count a 3-finger width per portion. For 6, I purchase the entire side, weighing in at about 2lbs (1kg). You could also use 4 to 6 skin-on salmon fillets, preferably center-cut pieces (6 to 8oz/170 to 225g each).

Two oven-roasting options

1

- Preheat your oven to 425°F (210°C)

- Place your side of salmon, skin side down, on a baking sheet. Drizzle lightly with olive oil, rub it right into the flesh, and then season generously with salt and pepper.

- Count on 8 to 10 minutes for every inch of thickness of the fish. Typically, I roast it for 15 minutes, but for a thicker piece you might want to go to 18.

- Remove from the oven, carefully slide the side of salmon onto a serving platter leaving the skin behind, and either spoon the sauce over the fish or pass it in a bowl at the table.

2

This is a method I discovered from cookbook author Mark Bittman, which is preferable if you like a crust on your fish.

- Preheat your oven to 475°F (240°C).

- Place a frying pan or flameproof roasting pan large enough to hold the side of salmon over medium high-heat and add 4 tablespoons (55g) butter. Scatter over some roughly chopped herbs like parsley or dill, if you like. When the butter is hot and starts to foam, place the salmon, skin side up, in the pan and sear, without moving it, for 1 minute. Place the pan in the oven and roast for 5 minutes. Remove from the oven and peel off the skin. Carefully turn the salmon over and then place the pan back in the oven for another 4 minutes, or 5 for a thicker piece. Transfer to a serving platter and serve with lemon wedges and the sauce alongside.

MANGO AND RED ONION SALSA

SERVES 4 TO 6

This recipe comes from my friend chef Roberto Santibañez, whose book *Truly Mexican* (Wiley, 2011) is my reference for modern Mexican cuisine. Fruit with salmon can be dicey, but this salsa is so well balanced that it works. I sometimes add some thin slices of red bell pepper to this as well.

1 large ripe (but firm) mango

3 tablespoons tequila

1 teaspoon sugar

2 or 3 medium tomatoes

½ cup finely sliced red onion (about 1 small onion)

1 tablespoon lime juice, plus more to taste

½ to 1 teaspoon salt

Freshly ground pepper to taste

2 teaspoons minced jalapeño or other red chili pepper, including seeds

2 tablespoons chopped cilantro

- Peel, pit, and finely dice the mango, then toss with the tequila and sugar in a small bowl and let macerate for 1 hour.

- Bring a small pot of water to a boil and prepare a bowl of ice water. Cut an X in the base of each tomato, then slide one into the boiling water and boil for 30 seconds. Immediately place in the ice water and repeat the operation with the other tomato(es). Once the tomatoes have cooled, remove from the water, peel off the skins, slice into quarters, remove the seeds, and roughly chop.

- Place the tomatoes in a medium bowl along with the onion, lime juice, salt, and pepper. Stir in the mango mixture, jalapeño (or other chili), and cilantro just before serving. Season with additional salt and lime juice to taste.

CHIMICHURRI

SERVES 4 TO 6

Often referred to as South American pesto, this vibrant sauce is primarily made of parsley (instead of pesto's basil) and comes in red and green versions. This is the green version, which is traditionally served with meat dishes in Argentina and Uruguay, but it also works brilliantly with chicken and fish.

2 to 3 tablespoons red wine vinegar

1/2 teaspoon salt

1/2 teaspoon freshly ground pepper

2 cups (about 3/4 of a bunch) Italian parsley, stems removed

2 to 4 garlic cloves, peeled

1/2 red chili (to make about 1 tablespoon minced), with seeds if you like it hot OR 1/2 teaspoon crushed red pepper flakes

1 tablespoon fresh oregano leaves OR 3/4 teaspoon dried oregano

1/2 cup (125ml) extra-virgin olive oil

- In a small bowl, whisk together 2 tablespoons vinegar, the salt, and pepper. Set aside.

- Finely chop the parsley, garlic, chili, and oregano. Place them in a bowl with the vinegar mixture and gradually whisk in the olive oil until well combined. For a tangier chimichurri, add the extra tablespoon of vinegar. Cover and let sit at room temperature for at least 1 hour before serving. Refrigerate any leftover sauce, covered, for up to a day.

Note: Chimichurri purists will surely protest, but in a pinch, you can also make this sauce in a blender or food processor, zapping it all together, save for the oil, which should be added in a stream at the end while the machine is running. The resulting sauce will have an emulsified, smooth texture not at all like the original but delicious just the same.

LOBSTER RISOTTO

Served at the peak of Canadian lobster season in spring and late fall, this luxurious risotto is a real treat. You can boil the lobsters in advance, or even buy them already cooked, but don't leave the meat in the shell for more than 2 days.

2 lobsters, approximately
1 ½lbs (675g) each

½ cup (135g) salt

Lobster Stock

2 tablespoons olive oil

Reserved carcasses of
the 2 lobsters

2 onions, quartered

2 celery stalks,
 coarsely chopped

2 tablespoons tomato paste

2 bay leaves

1 teaspoon peppercorns

About 4 cups (1L) water

$\longrightarrow$

- **Cook the lobsters:** Bring 5L of water and the salt to a boil in a lidded pot. Do not remove the rubber bands before cooking the lobsters. Drop the lobsters into the pot, heads down, cover, and boil for 9½ minutes (if cooking more than two lobsters, count the time once the water comes back to a boil). You can remove the lid halfway through cooking. Transfer the lobsters from the pot to a bowl and let cool slightly. Shell while hot, or rinse under cold water to cool the shells before proceeding. You'll end up with about 1½lb (300 to 360g) of meat in all. Keep the carcasses and refrigerate the meat.

- Heat the oil in a saucepan over high heat. Add the shells to the oil and sauté on all sides for a few minutes. Add the onions, celery, and tomato paste and sauté for a few more minutes. Add the bay leaves and peppercorns, then pour in enough cold water to cover by 1 inch (2.5 cm), at least 4 cups. Bring to a boil, skim off any impurities, reduce the heat to medium-low, and simmer for 90 minutes. Strain the stock into a saucepan and place it over medium heat.

$\longrightarrow$

(continued)

Risotto

2 tablespoons butter

2 shallots, minced

Salt and freshly ground pepper

¾ cup (160g) Arborio rice

about 3 cups (750ml) hot lobster stock (see previous step)

Reserved lobster meat (about 1½lbs/300 to 360g), cut into large pieces

Grated Parmesan cheese (optional)

Chopped chives or parsley for garnish

• Melt half the butter in a medium deep saucepan over medium-high heat. Add the shallots and cook until translucent. Season with salt and pepper, add the rice, and stir until the rice glistens. Begin ladling the hot broth over the rice, 1 cup at a time, and cook, stirring constantly and only adding more broth once the previous amount has been absorbed.

• After 20 minutes, the rice should be tender and creamy. Add the lobster pieces, the remaining butter, and Parmesan cheese to taste, if you like, and stir for another minute. The texture of a risotto should be creamy without being either too stiff or too liquid. Ideally it should spread out when spooned into a shallow bowl. If it seems a bit thick, add another ladleful of stock. Transfer to serving dishes and sprinkle with a bit of cheese, if you like, as well as the chives or parsley. Serve immediately.

ABOUT BOUILLABAISSE

Certain dishes are tied to a place because of ingredients specific to the area where it originated. Case in point, the famous Provençal stew/soup, bouillabaisse.

Originally from Marseilles and surrounding port villages, bouillabaisse consists of a garlic-and-saffron-infused fish broth in which fish are poached along with potatoes. The liquid must contain olive oil, which, when boiled rapidly, helps create an emulsion. Shellfish is optional, and the use of orange peel and fennel is always up for debate. As for consistency, an authentic bouillabaisse is thinner than your average restaurant fish soup.

Traditional accompaniments include sliced baguette (either stale or lightly toasted), garlic cloves (for rubbing on the bread), and rouille, an olive oil–emulsified spread made with potato, chili pepper, tomato, and saffron, as well as, in some versions, fresh almonds and/or garlic. About grated cheese atop the rouille, some say, "Yes please!" while authenticity sticklers would say, "Never!"

As much as I love a good bouillabaisse, it's challenging to re-create authentically on this side of the Atlantic, as the Mediterranean fish required in its makeup—the famous rascasse (scorpion fish), St. Peter's fish, red mullet, and an especially scary stinging specimen called a weever fish (la vive in French)—are next to impossible to find in Montreal. However, that doesn't mean we can't make bouillabaisse! Simply opt for local seafood and firm-fleshed fish (avoid oilier specimens), because not only is this fish stew a delicious and sensual dish, it's also ideal for a group.

For an extra-special occasion, pair it with a Provençal white wine or rosé. Because even if we can't get their fish, we can certainly drink their wine.

BOUILLABAISSE-INSPIRED FISH STEW

SERVES 6

I had to include a fish soup in this book because I ate my weight in them while reviewing restaurants, and also because it's an excellent one-pot meal, and not as difficult to make as you may think. If you can, prepare the fumet and the soup base a day ahead to help intensify the flavors. And if possible, keep the skin on the fish to help identify which ones you are eating when they are all served together.

¼ cup (60ml) olive oil

1½ cups chopped yellow onions (about 1½ medium onions)

1 small fennel bulb, trimmed and cut into small dice

3 tablespoons chopped garlic

2 cups (360g) diced tomatoes

1 tablespoon tomato paste

1 teaspoon fresh thyme leaves, minced

4 medium Yukon Gold potatoes, peeled and cut into large dice

½ teaspoon salt

½ teaspoon freshly ground pepper

2 teaspoons saffron threads

1 cup (250ml) dry white wine or white vermouth

4 cups (1L) Fish Fumet (p. 333)

½lb (225g) scallops, preferably diver

→

- **Make the soup base:** In a large soup pot or Dutch oven, heat the olive oil over medium heat and sauté the onions, fennel, and garlic until soft, about 5 minutes. Stir in the tomatoes, tomato paste, and thyme. Cook for 5 minutes more, then add the potatoes. Season with the salt and pepper and sprinkle over the saffron. Pour over the wine (or vermouth) and fish fumet and bring to a rolling boil, then reduce to a simmer for 10 minutes. Remove ¼ cup of the potato cubes and reserve for the rouille. At this point, the soup base can be cooled and refrigerated, then reheated right before serving.

- **To finish the soup:** Bring the soup base to a boil and let bubble for a couple of minutes. If the scallops are large, slice them in half. Add the clams and/or mussels, cover, and cook for 2 minutes. Add the fish and scallops, cover, and return to a gentle boil for 2 to 3 minutes. Add the shrimp for the last minute of the cooking time. Uncover and stir in the chopped herbs.

- **To serve:** Using a slotted spoon, remove the fish, seafood, and potatoes from the broth and place in a heated soup tureen, then carefully pour over the hot broth. Or serve the fish and seafood in a separate serving dish and the soup from the tureen. Distribute the fish and seafood evenly among separate serving bowls, place a few croutons spread with rouille in each,

→

(continued)

1 ½lbs (about 700g) clams or mussels OR a mix of both, scrubbed clean

1 ½lbs (about 700g) fish fillets, a mixture of 2 or 3 kinds of fish, such as monkfish, halibut, cod, hake, sea bass, and/or snapper, cut into large chunks

½lb (225g) shrimp (size 26–30)

2 to 3 tablespoons chopped fresh parsley, chervil, or tarragon

Rouille (recipe follows)

Croutons rubbed with garlic (about 3 per person) for serving

and ladle over some of the soup. Serve with extra bread and the rouille on the side.

- **Note:** For a slightly thicker soup: When you remove the fish, seafood, and vegetables from the broth, leave a few potatoes behind, and purée the broth with an immersion blender.

ROUILLE

Pinch of saffron threads

1/4 cup (60ml) warm
broth from the soup pot

2 garlic cloves

Pinch of salt

2 teaspoons minced
chili pepper

About 1/4 cup (50g) cooked
potatoes (from the broth)

1 egg yolk

1/3 cup (80ml) olive oil

Pinch of cayenne pepper

- Place the saffron in the warm broth to infuse.

- Chop the garlic cloves with the salt and chili to a paste. Place it in a blender with the potatoes and half of the broth and blend to make a smooth paste, then blend in the egg yolk. While the blender is running, slowly pour in the olive oil to emulsify. If the mixture is very thick, blend in the rest of the broth. Taste, and if you want more heat, add the pinch of cayenne. Transfer to a serving bowl and serve at once. Or cover and refrigerate; let come to room temperature for about 15 minutes before serving.

Note: Purists may balk at the addition of the egg yolk, saying, "A rouille is not a mayonnaise, Madame!" If you agree, leave it out. But I like the creamy texture that an egg yolk brings, and it also ensures that the sauce will not be too runny. I'll leave it up to you to decide.

SPOTLIGHT: L'EXPRESS, MY FAVORITE RESTAURANT

Of all the things Montreal is famous for, and on that list I'm including the Habs, the 1976 Olympics, and the Cirque de Soleil, I'm giving the top spot to our restaurant scene, because imagining my city without its restaurants would be difficult. And imagining Montreal without the St-Denis Street bistro L'Express would be impossible.

Not once have I walked past its cream-colored exterior and black-and-white checkered entranceway without yearning to go inside. And when I do go in, I relish every moment, slowly hanging my coat up on one of the hooks beside the door, turning around to scan the scene, looking for familiar staff members.

Opened in December 1980 by the late Colette Brossoit, her companion Pierre Villeneuve, and the late Luc Laporte, this old-school bistro is still going strong after some 45 years. The room has a comfortable timeworn noblesse, and beauty meets function in all the details: the zinc bar, the chocolate-colored walls, the paper-covered tabletops, the jar of cornichons atop every one. For that, the credit goes to Laporte, the architect/designer behind many of the city's most beautiful and enduring dining spaces.

Montreal is a French city, and the best place to witness that is at a crowded night at L'Express. In my early 20s, I was intimidated by the sheer Frenchness of it all. The maitre d' was haughty, the wine list was overwhelming, and what the heck was a Toulouse frites anyway? Now, some 30 years later, I'm continuously seduced by its Gallic charm.

A night at L'Express is an escape, a sort of quick jaunt to Paris without the luggage or jet lag. Yet it's Paris sans the stressed-out Parisians, for the staff appears to have softened around the edges. Today's maitre d' is welcoming and the apron-clad servers are all smiles. From the best tables around the palm tree midroom, or against the south wall under the large mirrors, you can watch this movie set of a dining room in full action. But for a tête-a-tête, patrons willingly turn their backs to the crowd for a more intimate evening at the bar.

L'Express's menu has often been described in two words: reliable and consistent—both true and admirable, considering this restaurant often serves up to 500 covers a day. The food's not flashy or wildly creative, but boy, is it ever good. Bistro fare is the original French comfort food. Anything fancier, and you've missed the point.

Regulars—and there are many—have their favorites. For some it's the fish soup, for others it's the grilled salmon or kidneys with mustard sauce. For me, it's the sorrel soup, and the quail with wild rice and peas. Their best-selling dish is the onglet frites, served not with ketchup but with a mustardy mayonnaise. For dessert, I'm faithful to the lemon tart, but many prefer the massive île flottante.

The wine is another big draw. With some 11,000 bottles on offer, this "carte" features privately imported bottles chosen simply for being good, affordable, and festive. (Insider tip: ask about their secret second wine list with limited-availability bottles).

Busier, noisier, and chicer than most, this deservedly famous bistro is all about pleasure and enjoying a good time in a truly convivial atmosphere. More than just another great Montreal restaurant, L'Express has captured the essence of the city itself.

Meat and Poultry

BOEUF CAROTTES

SERVES 6 TO 8

This dish resembles boeuf bourguignon yet avoids all the finicky garnishes and puts the focus as much on the carrots as the meat. Feel free to up the number of carrots if you prefer, and serve the dish with mashed potatoes or, my preference, a big bowl of buttered egg noodles. Pair it with a fine red wine, and you have a dinner party dish.

2.2 to 2.8lbs (1 to 1.3kg) chuck roast or flat-iron steak

1 25oz (750ml) bottle naturally carbonated water

Salt and freshly ground pepper

2 tablespoons vegetable oil

1 large red or yellow onion, thinly sliced

2 carrots, diced

1 large garlic clove, chopped

1 tablespoon tomato paste

2 tablespoons toasted flour*

2 cups (500ml) red wine

2 cups (500ml) beef broth

A few sprigs fresh thyme

1 sprig fresh rosemary

2 bay leaves

1¾lbs (about 800g) carrots

A handful of parsley leaves, roughly chopped

- Cut the beef into 2-inch (5 cm) cubes, removing any excess fat or sinew. Place in a large bowl and pour over the sparkling water to cover. Let sit at room temperature for 1 hour. This step is optional, but it will help tenderize the meat.

- Preheat your oven to 325°F (160°C). Drain the beef cubes and pat them dry with paper towels. Season with salt and pepper on all sides.

- In a large Dutch oven, heat 1½ tablespoons of the oil over high heat. Once the oil begins to smoke, add half the cubes of meat and sear on all sides. Don't crowd the pot, and only turn the pieces when they easily release when lifted. You want them nicely browned. Transfer them to a plate and repeat the operation with the other half of the beef cubes and set them aside.

- Add the remaining ½ tablespoon of oil to the pot and then add the onions, diced carrots, and garlic. Reduce the heat to medium-high and stir until the vegetables are cooked through. Stir in the tomato paste and cook for another minute, then add the beef cubes back to the pot. Sprinkle over the browned flour, then stir everything together until the flour disappears. Pour over the wine, bring to a rolling boil, and flambé it (if you're up to it). When the flames have subsided, pour in the beef broth. Stir to combine everything, add the herbs, cover, and place in the oven.

- Meanwhile, prepare your carrots: If they are very fresh, there's no need to peel them. Just slice off the greens and scrape off any dark spots. Rinse and set aside.

- After 2 hours of braising time, add the carrots in a single layer over the top of the beef stew, sprinkle with salt, cover the pot, and braise for another hour.

- After the third hour, check the beef and carrots to see if they're done. The beef should be very tender, and the carrots should be cooked through. If not, place the pot back in the oven for another 15 to 30 minutes.

- When ready to serve, dish up the beef on a platter. If the sauce appears to be very thick, stir in a bit of water and bring to a boil, then pour it over the meat and arrange a few carrots decoratively over the top. Sprinkle with the parsley and serve immediately.

***Note for the toasted flour:** Place your flour in a small frying pan over medium heat and stir it until it begins to turn brown. Continue stirring until the flour is a uniform golden color. Any extra flour can be stored in a closed container and used for making gravies and other savory sauces.

POULET DU BEAU-FRÈRE
(BROTHER-IN-LAW'S CHICKEN)

My brother-in-law, Philippe, is an excellent cook and, as he is Parisian, has very strong ideas about the way he likes his food (no sweet and savory on the same plate, no hot and cold items together . . . ; you get the picture). When it comes to French food, he is a stickler, and when it comes to chicken dishes, he is a master. His take on the classic Poulet Grand-Mère is my favorite of his dishes. I love it so much, I ate three portions the first time he served it. Pair with a nice Beaujolais.

Salt

1 roasting chicken, about 5lbs (2.25kg)

1½ tablespoons vegetable oil, divided

2½ tablespoons butter, divided

1 shallot

1 medium carrot

1 small yellow onion

1 garlic clove, unpeeled

A few sprigs fresh thyme

1½ cups (375ml) dry white wine, divided

12 medium new potatoes or 18 small ones (peeled if you like)

15 to 20 pearl onions, peeled

1 8oz (224g) container button mushrooms

5oz (150g) thick-cut bacon, cubed

- Preheat the oven to 500°F (250°C) and set an oven rack to the lowest position. Salt the chicken inside and out.

- Heat a large cast-iron Dutch oven (such as Staub or Le Creuset) over medium-high heat. Add a tablespoon each of oil and butter, and when the butter begins to foam, brown the chicken on all 4 sides, allowing about 3 minutes per side. If the oil at the bottom of the pot is very dark, pour most of it out. Place the chicken in the oven, uncovered, for 10 minutes.

- Meanwhile, cut the shallot, carrot, and onion into a mirepoix (small dice).

- Remove the pot from the oven and add the mirepoix, garlic clove, and thyme, stirring a little, then deglaze with 1 cup (250ml) white wine. Turn the oven down to 450°F (220°C) and return the pot to the oven, this time covered. Roast the chicken for about 50 minutes, basting every 15 minutes.

- While the chicken is in the oven, steam the potatoes and keep warm.

- Prepare the garnish: Bring a small pan of water to a boil, plunge in the pearl onions, and cook for 5 minutes. Drain and set aside.

Freshly ground pepper
to taste

1 cup (250ml) unsalted veal
or chicken stock

A handful of parsley leaves,
coarsely chopped

- Quickly rinse the mushrooms and then wipe clean, then cut into quarters. Heat a medium frying pan over high heat, add the remaining $1/2$ tablespoon oil and $1/2$ tablespoon butter, add the mushrooms, and sauté until golden. Remove to a plate and set aside.

- Add the bacon to the same pan and brown. Remove the bacon with a slotted spoon and set aside, leaving the fat in the pan. Reduce the heat to low and sauté the pearl onions in the bacon fat (be careful not to burn them!). Set aside.

- **To serve:** Once the chicken is cooked, remove from the pot to a plate and cover lightly with aluminum foil to rest. Return the casserole to high heat, deglaze with the remaining $1/2$ cup white wine, and reduce for a few minutes. Add the veal (or chicken) stock and reduce for about 5 minutes. Taste the sauce, and season with salt and pepper to taste.

- Cut the chicken into 8 pieces (or as desired) and arrange them on a warmed serving platter. Scatter the bacon, onions, and mushrooms around the chicken. Sauté the potatoes in the last tablespoon of butter in a frying pan and serve alongside.

- Ladle the sauce from the pot over the chicken (removing the garlic clove), sprinkle with parsley, and serve immediately.

GRILLED LEG OF LAMB

SERVES 8

This lamb, served with ratatouille and a good red or rosé, is my favorite summertime feast.
I use Quebec lamb from the region of Charlevoix on the north shore of the Saint Lawrence
River for this recipe when available, but New Zealand lamb also works well. Ask your
butcher to bone and butterfly the leg, remove excess fat, and pound it to an even thickness.
I would recommend using a thermometer when grilling to avoid over- or undercooking.

¾ cup (180ml) olive oil

1 cup (250ml) full-bodied
red wine

1 large head of garlic,
cloves separated, peeled,
and roughly chopped

2 tablespoons chopped
fresh rosemary

2 tablespoons chopped
fresh thyme

1½ teaspoons salt

1½ teaspoons coarsely
ground pepper

1 leg of lamb (about
4.5lbs/2kg)

1 large lemon

- **For the marinade:** In a medium bowl, mix the olive oil,
  red wine, garlic, rosemary, thyme, salt, and pepper.
  Place the lamb in a baking dish just a bit smaller than
  the meat (it should fit snugly). Pour the marinade
  over the top, then turn it over to allow the marinade
  to coat all sides. Feel free to give it a rub. Cover with
  plastic wrap and refrigerate for a day, turning the lamb
  occasionally.

- **To grill:** Remove the meat from the refrigerator about
  an hour before grilling. Lift it from the marinade and
  lightly pat dry, leaving some of the garlic and herbs
  clinging to it. A boned leg of lamb can be unruly.
  To secure the meat, insert 4 long metal skewers (2
  lengthwise and 2 crosswise) through the lamb, pushing
  any smaller flaps toward the center. Skewering the
  lamb this way is optional but also helps promote even
  cooking.

- On a lightly oiled grill grate set about 6 inches (15 cm)
  above glowing coals, grill the lamb for about 10 minutes
  on each side. For medium-rare, the lamb should register
  130°F (55°C) on an instant-read thermometer inserted
  into the thickest part of the meat. Alternatively, roast
  the lamb in a roasting pan in the middle of a 425°F
  (220°C) oven for about 30 minutes.

- Transfer the lamb to a cutting board. Cut the lemon
  in half, remove the seeds, and squeeze the juice over
  the lamb. Let stand, loosely covered with foil, for 15
  minutes. Cut the lamb into thin slices and serve with
  any juices that have accumulated on the cutting board.

RATATOUILLE

SERVES 4 TO 6

I often make a version of ratatouille by grilling all the vegetables and assembling
them as a salad. This recipe, however, is for the real-deal Provençal vegetable stew
that is traditionally served as a side dish for meat, especially lamb. But don't stop
there. You can use it as a pasta sauce, layer it in a lasagna, or spoon it into the base
of a quiche. It's also delicious when puréed and eaten as a vegetable soup.

1 large eggplant

Salt

2 medium red onions

2 medium green zucchini

1 large red bell pepper

3 medium tomatoes

A few sprigs of thyme

1 bay leaf

2 garlic cloves, peeled
and thinly sliced

About 1/4 cup (60ml)
olive oil

Freshly ground pepper

About 6 fresh basil leaves

- Peel the eggplant if you like (not necessary) and cut into
  cubes. The cubes can be any size you like, but try to cut
  all the vegetables the same size. Season generously with
  salt, toss, and leave in a bowl for 30 minutes.

- Meanwhile, peel the onions and cut into large cubes.
  Trim the ends of the zucchini and dice too. Under the
  broiler or directly on a gas burner, grill the bell pepper
  all over until blackened. Wrap in a paper towel and
  leave to cool, then rub it with the paper towel to remove
  the skin. Cut in half, scoop out the seeds, and slice into
  large dice. Plunge the tomatoes in boiling water for 30
  seconds, rinse them in cold water, then remove the skins
  and cut into quarters.

- Place the tomatoes, thyme, bay leaf, and garlic in a large
  pot or Dutch oven and stir over medium heat until the
  tomatoes turn to mush. Let bubble away and reduce,
  stirring from time to time, to make a sauce.

- In a large frying pan over medium heat, add half the oil
  and sauté the onions and bell pepper for a few minutes.
  Transfer them to the pot with the tomatoes and return
  the pan to the heat, with the remaining oil. Add the
  zucchini, stir well, and cover the pan for 5 minutes.

- Meanwhile, squeeze the eggplant firmly between your fingers, then wrap in a paper towel to remove any excess liquid. Add it to the pan with the zucchini, stir well, and cook until all the vegetables are tender and starting to caramelize slightly.

- Transfer the zucchini and eggplant to the pot with the tomato sauce, mix well, and season with salt and pepper. Simmer over medium-low heat for a further 20 minutes, stirring occasionally, until the mixture is smooth. Add a little water if it looks too dry.

- **To serve:** Remove the bay leaf and thyme sprigs, roughly tear the basil leaves, and stir them into the stew.

LAMB SHANKS WITH PRUNES AND SPICES

SERVES 4

This delicious lamb stew is lightly spiced, lightly sweetened, and deeply
flavored. The recipe is adapted from a dish by chef Mohand Yahiaoui,
owner of Les Rites Berbères restaurant in Montreal.

4 lamb shanks, about 1 lb
(450g) each

Salt and freshly ground
pepper

2 tablespoons extra-virgin
olive oil

1 large Spanish onion, finely
chopped

4 large garlic cloves, finely
chopped

2 cups pitted prunes

2 large pinches saffron
threads

1/2 teaspoon finely ground
coriander seeds

1/2 teaspoon ground cumin

1 1/2 teaspoons ground
ginger

1/2 stick cinnamon

2 2-inch-long strips
orange peel

3 cups (750ml) chicken
broth, preferably homemade,
OR 2 cups (450ml) broth
and 1 cup (250ml) of the
prune soaking water

- Pat the lamb shanks dry and season with salt and
pepper. In a deep frying pan or cast-iron saucepan (such
as Le Creuset), heat the olive oil over medium-high
heat, add the shanks, and sear on all sides to brown.
Remove the shanks and set aside.

- Add the onions to the hot pan, stir well, and add a pinch
of salt. Reduce the heat to medium, cover, and simmer
for about 10 minutes, stirring occasionally, until the
onions melt considerably. Remove the lid, stir in the
chopped garlic, and sauté until golden.

- Meanwhile, place the prunes in a bowl and cover with
boiling water. Leave to soften for 15 minutes, then
drain, reserving the soaking water (alternatively, they
can be steamed for 15 minutes, which will make them
even softer).

- Add the spices to the onions and stir until they are well
incorporated. Return the shanks to the pan, turn them
over in the onions, and then gently stir in the prunes
and orange zest. Pour the broth (or the broth and prune
water) into the pan and bring to a boil, then stir in the
honey. Cover and leave to simmer over low heat for
about 2 hours, or until the meat is tender. (Alternatively,
place the pan in an oven preheated to 325° F/160°C for
about 2 1/2 hours, or until the meat is fork-tender.)

2 tablespoons honey

¹/4 cup (25g) toasted
slivered almonds

2 tablespoons toasted
sesame seeds

Couscous to serve

- When the stew is ready, taste the braising juices to adjust the seasonings. Remove the shanks to a serving bowl. If the sauce is too thin, you can reduce it until it just begins to coat the back of a spoon. Ladle the sauce over the lamb, sprinkle with the toasted almonds and sesame seeds, and serve immediately, with couscous alongside.

PAN-SEARED DUCK WITH CHERRIES

SERVES 4

As duck farms are plentiful in Quebec, there's no way you can talk about Montreal cuisine without a mention of duck foie gras, confit, or the breasts of fattened ducks, known as magrets. Duck in some form is featured on most Montreal restaurant menus, and at home I serve it on special occasions with a potato and cauliflower gratin, asparagus when in season, and a serious bottle of Pinot Noir.

4 duck breasts, about ½lb (225g) each, OR 2 duck magrets, about 1lb (450g) each

Salt and freshly ground pepper

1 19oz (540ml) jar sour cherries in light syrup (not maraschino cherries)*

1 cup (250ml) red wine

2 tablespoons brown sugar

2 whole star anise

1 piece fresh ginger, about 2 inches (5 cm) in size

1 2-inch-long strip orange peel

- Pat the duck breasts dry, then lightly score them with a sharp knife on the skin side in a crosshatch pattern, only piercing about ¼ inch (½ cm) of the skin (this will prevent the skin from shrinking back when cooking). Season liberally with salt and pepper, rubbing it right into the skin, then set aside at room temperature until ready to cook.

- Drain the cherries, reserving the syrup. Measure out 1 cup of the syrup and 1 cup of the cherries. Pour the remaining syrup and cherries back into the jar and refrigerate for future use.

- Set the drained cherries aside and pour the cup of cherry syrup into a medium saucepan, along with the wine, brown sugar, star anise, ginger, and orange peel. Bring the mixture to a boil, stir, reduce to a simmer, and continue to cook until the liquid thickens to a maple syrup–like consistency. You should end up with about ½ cup (125ml). Turn off the heat, remove the star anise pods, ginger, and orange peel, and let cool slightly. Pour about 2 tablespoons of the syrup into a ramekin. You'll use this to glaze the duck.

- Preheat your oven to 325°F (160°C). Place the seasoned duck breasts, skin side down, in an ovenproof frying pan, then place the pan over medium heat. Fry the

$\longrightarrow$

(continued)

breasts, without touching or turning them, for about 10 minutes, until the skin is a deep and even golden color. Remove the breasts from the pan and pour off all but a few spoonfuls of the fat. Place the duck back in the hot pan, skin side up, and brush half the glaze generously over the skin. Place the pan in the oven. Roast for 10 minutes, basting the breasts with the remaining glaze after 5 minutes of cooking. Remove from the oven, place on a plate, tent lightly with aluminum foil, and let rest for at least 10 minutes (you want the duck to relax and the pinkness to spread throughout the meat).

- Meanwhile, heat the reserved syrup in the pan over medium heat until it comes to a boil. Add the reserved cherries and swirl them around in the syrup to reduce the sauce a bit and warm the cherries through.

- **To serve:** Cut the duck breasts into thin slices and fan them out on a serving platter. Whisk any accumulated juices from the meat into the cherry sauce, then pour it over the slices right before serving.

***Note:** If you cannot find jarred cherries in syrup, you can make your own: Boil together 1 cup (240ml) of water and $1/4$ cup (50g) sugar. Add $2^1/_2$ cups (500g) fresh or frozen pitted sour cherries. Boil everything together for 30 seconds and remove from the heat.

GRATIN SAVOYARD WITH CAULIFLOWER

SERVES 4 TO 6

Though many would call this a Gratin Dauphinois, a Dauphinois does not include cheese and often includes an egg in the filling. A Gratin Savoyard is the one with a cheese topping, and the addition of cauliflower makes for a—somewhat—lighter dish. For a special treat, add some sautéed chanterelles between the layers.

1 garlic clove, peeled and halved

Salt

4 medium Yukon Gold or Russet potatoes (1¾lbs/800g total)

½ small or ¼ large head cauliflower (about ½lb/225g)

1 cup (250ml) whipping cream

1½ cups (375ml) milk, divided

¼ teaspoon nutmeg

¼ teaspoon freshly ground pepper, preferably white

1 cup (100g) grated Gruyère or Cheddar cheese

- Preheat your oven to 325°F (160°C). Have ready a 9 by 13-inch (23 by 33 cm) gratin dish (or one around that size). Sprinkle the garlic with salt and then rub the cut side against the base and sides of the dish. Set aside.

- Peel the potatoes and then, using a mandoline slicer or a knife, slice into rounds about ⅛-inch-thick (3 mm). Place in a kitchen towel and pat dry. Slice the cauliflower a bit thicker than the potatoes.

- In a large pot or deep frying pan, bring the cream and 1¼ cups (285ml) milk to a boil with the nutmeg, 1 teaspoon salt, the pepper, and the pieces of garlic. Add the potatoes, bring back to a boil, add the cauliflower, and add the remaining ¼ cup of milk. Reduce to a simmer for about 5 minutes and then transfer the entire mix to the gratin dish. Sprinkle over the cheese and bake for about 30 minutes, or until the top is golden and everything is bubbling. Let sit for about 5 minutes to cool a bit before serving.

ABOUT CASSOULET

If ever there was a bistro dish I yearned to re-create in my home kitchen, it was always cassoulet. But what, you may be asking, exactly is cassoulet?

Dubbed "the God" of Southwestern French cuisine by none other than gastronome Prosper Montagné, cassoulet is essentially a bean stew. Not just any bean stew, mind you, but a lush ragout of braised beans enriched with duck or goose confit, pork parts, and Toulouse or andouillette sausages. Mutton is common in more northern recipes of the region, and the inclusion of gizzards and pork skin points to cassoulet's humble origins. Cassoulet can have a toasted bread-crumb crust, or not. Some are enhanced with tomato, while others are enriched with duck stock and pork fat.

Toulouse, Carcassonne, and the village of Castelnaudary are the towns most famous for their cassoulet. Each location lays claim to the original recipe, though Castelnaudary is generally acknowledged as the birthplace of the dish. Named for the clay pot in which it is baked, a cassole, cassoulet can today be found the world over on practically any serious French bistro menu.

A 1966 decree drawn up by the États Généraux de la Gastronomie Française states that a cassoulet should be 30 percent pork or other meat and 70 percent beans, stock, and seasonings. As they make up three-quarters of the dish, the beans are the key to a successful cassoulet. Ideally, they should be simmered, holding their shape, just until the moment they are served. As for the taste, long braising ensures that their gentle earthiness will be well infused with their surrounding meats and fats.

Though cassoulet is best served in cold weather, I do recall a chef telling me that he and his brother had a ritual of devouring plates of cassoulet in Toulouse each summer, wearing only their underwear, sweating profusely.

The first time I made cassoulet, it took me 3 days to assemble. And when I finally sat down to eat it, I was too wiped to enjoy all that work. If, like me, the idea of patiently assembling a cassoulet makes you quiver, consider this recipe.

QUICK CASSOULET

SERVES 8

The idea that the famous Southwestern French dish, cassoulet, can be quick is a bit of a stretch, as it usually takes days to prepare from start to finish. But if you use precooked products—I rely on store-bought duck confit and canned beans—and prepare them in the style of a cassoulet (and give them some time to bake and meld together), you'll come quite close.

4 duck confit legs, about 1/2lb (225g) each

3 19oz (540ml) cans cannellini beans (white kidney beans)

1 medium onion, chopped fine

3 medium carrots, peeled and cut into thin rounds

2 garlic cloves, peeled and chopped

1/4lb (110g) kielbasa or pancetta, diced

2 tablespoons tomato paste

3 sprigs each fresh parsley and thyme

2 bay leaves

2 1/4 cups (560ml) chicken or vegetable broth

4 Toulouse sausages

1/3 cup (40g) breadcrumbs

- Heat your oven to 325°F (160°C). Have ready a large deep frying pan or a 12-inch (30 cm) Dutch oven.

- Remove the duck confit from its jar or packaging, setting aside as much fat as you can remove, as well as any jelled broth. Remove all the meat from the bones in large pieces (it's up to you whether you keep the skin) and set aside too. Drain and rinse the canned beans. You should end up with just over 2lbs (900g) of beans.

- In a large deep frying pan or Dutch oven over medium-high heat, melt 3 tablespoons of the duck fat you set aside, and when it's hot, add the chopped onion. Sauté for a minute, then add the carrots, followed by the garlic and diced kielbasa (or pancetta). Sauté until everything is softened, then stir in the tomato paste. Continue to sauté until the paste begins to caramelize. Add the beans and stir to coat them with the vegetables.

- Remove half the beans from the pan (or pot), spread the remaining beans out in an even layer, and add the parsley and thyme sprigs, as well as the bay leaves. Scatter the duck meat evenly over the top, as well as any of the reserved jelled broth. Add the rest of the beans, spreading them into an even layer over the duck, and then pour the stock over the top, to come at least halfway up the sides of the beans. Bring to a boil, then place the pan (or pot) in the oven and bake, uncovered, for 1 hour.

$\longrightarrow$

(continued)

- Meanwhile, grill or fry the sausages until well colored on the outside but not cooked through. Let cool, then slice them in half, lengthwise.

- After an hour of cooking time, remove the pan (or pot) from the oven, give the beans a good stir, and then even them out once again. Place the sausage halves over the top, pressing down to submerge them halfway into the stew. Sprinkle the crumbs over the top and bake for another 30 minutes. Remove from the oven and let sit for about 15 minutes before serving.

Note: Cassoulet reheats very well and is even better the day after—or several days after—it is made.

COOKING WITH YOUR SENSES

As much as I recommend strictly following a recipe the first time you give it a go, it's equally important to trust your senses when you cook.

Taste is no doubt the most relied upon of the five senses for a cook. But when you think about it, they all come into play: the feel of a dough that's too wet or dry as it's kneaded, the look of onions when they become translucent as they cook, the sound of a stew as it bubbles and thickens on a low simmer, the smell of brownies when they are baked . . .

Such instincts are not heightened overnight. You'll have to fry a good number of pork chops before knowing whether the sound of the meat hitting the pan indicates the right temperature. I've had to roll out hundreds of rounds of pie dough to be able to gauge whether or not the thickness is correct by touch. It's not the obvious things that elude us—we all know what burned rice smells like and a runny pie filling looks like—but the more subtle observations that separate the novice cooks from the experts.

An experienced cook can tell whether pasta is cooked not by throwing a strand of spaghetti against the wall, but by the feel of the wooden spoon touching the pasta while stirring. Want to know whether your cake is baked? You can rely on a toothpick coming out clean, but try pressing down on the surface, and if it springs back, it's done. You can use a meat thermometer to check whether your steak is medium-rare, but most chefs will press on the meat to judge the level of firmness (the firmer the meat, the closer it is to well done).

In cooking school, a teacher taught me to not bother with a timer for cookies but to check them once their odor filled the room. He also taught me that the best way to determine whether cream puffs are cooked is to place one next to your ear. If you hear it sizzling, he explained, it'll need to be baked a bit longer. Try it, it works!

I would even add a sixth sense to this list: the sense of time. A trained cook can have many tasks going at once but will instinctively know when to pull that tray of croutons out of the oven, stop steaming the Brussels sprouts before they go gray, and turn off the mixer so that the whipped cream doesn't turn to butter— often at the same time!

Make it a goal as you improve your cooking to start trusting your senses to help guide you, and eventually you won't need to set the timer for cookies, cakes, or even broccoli. Salting a soup will simply become part of the process. And dressing a salad just until it glistens with—not drowns in—vinaigrette is what will lift you from good cook to great.

A Curry Feast

If there's one meal I consider the ultimate feast, it's an Indian curry. An Indian curry from a Montreal cook? Yes! Let me explain.

My family isn't Indian, but my father, like so many Brits, could have eaten curry every day, and thanks to the many Indian restaurants in downtown Montreal, he often did. Every time we visited a French, Italian, Greek, or other restaurant, I knew my dad would rather be at his favorite Indian restaurant in Montreal, Le Taj.

Not to be outdone, my mother began adding curries to her culinary repertoire, opening the door for the whole family to discover Indian cuisine and the immense joy it brings. Following the recipes of the grande dame of Indian cooking, Madhur Jaffrey, and the wonderful book *Foods of the World: India* published by Time-Life, she prepared curries with shrimp, lamb, and vegetables, but her chicken curry was always my favorite.

Of course, there's a lot more to a curry feast than a simple chicken curry. Accompaniments are essential to any Indian meal and, though the ingredients lists are lengthy, most Indian side dishes are simple to prepare. Basmati rice is a must, as is a dal, a sort of split pea porridge flavored with onions, garlic, ginger, and spices. A yogurt dish is essential at a curry dinner to help neutralize the chilies and strong spices. My choice is always a raita, made by mixing the cooling, fruity flavors of cucumber, tomato, and cilantro into yogurt.

Also enjoyable are the hot and/or sweet flavors of pickled vegetables and mango chutney, which I usually buy ready-made. When choosing from the many varieties of bottled chutney, be sure to reach for a sweet one like Major Grey, and a spicy condiment, such as hot mango pickle laced with mustard-seed oil.

Flatbreads are also key when eating Indian. Pappadums, a delicious flatbread made from chickpea flour, can easily be found in large supermarkets or specialty stores and fried (or toasted) in no time. Right before serving, heat an inch of oil in a small frying pan, add the thin disks of raw pappadum dough, and watch them billow up into enormous crunchy tuiles. I also serve homemade naan bread at the table because it's simple to make and is perfect for soaking up every last drop of sauce. I sometimes add little bowls of toasted coconut or cashews to sprinkle over the dishes before we start. And I always have a green chutney to add sizzle to my plate.

For dessert, I like slices of mango drizzled with lime or a thick slice of kulfi, that fragrant frozen dessert.

And finally, to drink . . . My father always opted for a beer (a Double Diamond, to be precise), but for a more refined meal, I accompany the curry with wine. A sparkling rosé, a Riesling, or a Gewürztraminer is just the thing.

MOM'S CHICKEN CURRY

SERVES 6

Over the years, my mother adapted her chicken curry, basically upping the spices
and reducing the amount of oil, based on Murg Kari's recipe published in 1969
in the book *Foods of the World: India*, from the Time-Life cookbook series.

1 5lb (2.5kg) chicken, cut into 10 pieces, skin removed but not boned, as well as 2 extra thighs, legs, or wings (also skinned), if desired

1 tablespoon salt, divided

2 teaspoons ground cumin

2 teaspoons ground turmeric

2 teaspoons ground coriander

2 to 3 teaspoons cayenne pepper (depending on how hot you like it)

1 teaspoon ground fennel

1/4 cup (60ml) vegetable oil

3 cups finely chopped yellow onions (about 2 medium onions)

2 tablespoons finely chopped garlic

2 tablespoons finely chopped or grated fresh ginger

1 cup (250ml) water

1 14oz (398ml) can chopped tomatoes

- Lay the chicken pieces on a layer of paper towels, pat dry, and sprinkle all over with half the salt. Set aside while you toast the spices.

- Combine the cumin, turmeric, coriander, cayenne pepper, and fennel in a small frying pan and toast over low heat, stirring slowly, until the spices become fragrant. Remove from the heat and set aside.

- In a large heavy frying pan or a Dutch oven, heat the oil over high heat. Add the chicken pieces (swirling them a bit in the oil as you place them in the pan) and fry them on all sides until lightly golden and firm. Avoid crowding the pieces, and do not turn them over too quickly, or you will rip the flesh. Do this in 2 or 3 batches, reducing the heat if necessary, and transferring the pieces to a platter as you go.

- When all the chicken is browned, reduce the heat to medium-high and add the onions, garlic, and ginger all at once. Stirring constantly, sauté for about 5 minutes, or until the onions are soft and beginning to turn an even golden brown.

- Reduce the heat to medium-low and stir in the toasted spices, as well as a few spoonfuls of the water, and cook for a minute. Stir in the tomatoes, half the cilantro, and the yogurt, along with the remaining salt. Add the chicken pieces and any accumulated juices and

About ¹/₂ cup chopped
cilantro

1 cup (250ml) plain yogurt
(not Greek-style)

1 tablespoon garam masala

¹/₂ lemon

increase the heat to medium. Pour in the remaining water, bring the mixture to a boil, stir to make sure the chicken pieces are coated in the sauce, and sprinkle over the garam masala. Reduce the heat to a simmer, cover tightly, and cook for 20 minutes, or until the chicken is tender but not falling apart (if it is, don't worry, it will still be great).

- **To serve:** Arrange the chicken pieces on a serving platter. If the sauce looks a bit thin, you can reduce it over high heat to thicken it. Then spoon the sauce over the chicken, sprinkle over the remaining cilantro, and squeeze over the lemon.

RAITA

MAKES ABOUT 1 ½ CUPS (375ML)

This cooling yogurt sauce is a must with curry, not only to provide a bit of relief from the hot curry, but also to add a contrasting texture and temperature to the plate.

½ English cucumber (peeled or not)

1 tablespoon finely chopped shallot

1 teaspoon salt, or more to taste

1 ½ cups (375ml) plain yogurt (not Greek-style)

1 medium tomato, diced

¼ cup (4g) chopped fresh cilantro

1 teaspoon toasted ground cumin

1 teaspoon chopped chives (optional)

- Slice the cucumber in half lengthwise, scoop out the seeds, and either cut it into a small dice or grate it on the largest holes of a box grater. Toss the cucumber together with the shallot and salt in a bowl, and set aside for 5 minutes, then wrap it in a paper towel and squeeze out as much of the accumulated liquid as possible.

- Place the cucumber mix in a serving bowl, along with the yogurt, tomato, cilantro, and cumin, and stir to combine. Taste and add more salt if needed. Sprinkle with the chopped chives and refrigerate, covered, until ready to serve.

GREEN CHUTNEY

MAKES 1 CUP (250ML)

1 cup (about 30g) fresh mint leaves

1 cup (about 16g) roughly chopped cilantro, leaves and stems

2 scallions, chopped

1 garlic clove, peeled and chopped

1 2-inch (5 cm) piece fresh ginger, peeled and chopped

½ hot green chili, chopped

Juice of ½ lemon or 1 lime

¼ cup (60ml) warm water

1 teaspoon salt

1 tablespoon vegetable oil

½ teaspoon ground cumin

- Place all the ingredients in a blender and process until you reach a fine consistency. Transfer to a small bowl and cover with plastic wrap placed right against the surface of the sauce; refrigerate until ready to serve.

YELLOW DAL

This comforting vegetarian side dish is, as cookbook author Madhur Jaffrey says,
"the core" of an Indian meal. This recipe was given to me years ago at a cooking
class at Poppadoms restaurant in Kelowna, BC. Spoon the dal generously
onto your plates; any leftovers can be enjoyed over rice the next day.

1 ½ cups (275g) red lentils

5 ¼ cups (1.3L) water

1 teaspoon turmeric

2 teaspoons vegetable oil

1 teaspoon cumin seeds

1 teaspoon mustard seeds

1 small onion or large
shallot, finely chopped

2 teaspoons salt, divided

1 teaspoon finely
chopped garlic

1 teaspoon grated
fresh ginger

½ teaspoon chili powder

1 small tomato, finely
chopped

1 teaspoon garam masala

Chopped cilantro to garnish

- Rinse the lentils thoroughly in plenty of cold water, about 5 times, until the water runs clear. Place the lentils in a saucepan with the water, bring to a boil (be careful it doesn't boil over), reduce the heat to medium, and skim off any foam as it accumulates. Add the turmeric once all the foam has been removed and cook at a simmer for 45 minutes, stirring occasionally.

- Meanwhile, heat the oil in a small frying pan over medium-high heat, then add the cumin and mustard seeds and let sizzle and pop for a few seconds. Add the onion (or shallot) along with a teaspoon of salt and sauté until softened. Stir in the garlic, ginger, chili powder, and tomato and cook until the mixture forms a paste. Remove from the heat.

- When the lentils are cooked, add the remaining teaspoon of salt and stir in the paste and the garam masala. Bring back to a boil and, for an even smoother dal, give it a brisk whisk. Transfer to a serving dish and garnish with a bit of chopped cilantro.

BASIC BASMATI

This is the easiest rice recipe to make, it's ready in 10 minutes,
and it can be served alongside most anything.

1 ½ cups (300g) best-quality basmati rice

3 cups (720ml) water

Large pinch of salt

1 tablespoon butter

- Rinse your rice in a bowl of cold water several times, until the water runs clear.

- In a medium lidded pot, bring the water to a boil. Add the rice, salt, and butter and stir once with a fork to distribute the grains. Bring back to a boil, reduce the heat to low, cover, and set your timer for 10 minutes. Have a thin cotton napkin or two thicknesses of paper towel at the ready.

- When the time is up, uncover the pot. You should see tunnels in the rice where the steam is escaping. Push the rice to one side to see whether there is any liquid remaining. If there is, continue cooking for a few minutes more.

- When all the liquid has been absorbed, turn off the heat, remove the lid, gently fluff up the rice, place the napkin (or paper towels) over the pot, and place the lid back on. Allow to sit for a minute or two (or until you are ready to serve) so that the napkin captures the steam, which will prevent the rice from getting sticky.

- Uncover, fluff up the rice once again, and transfer to a serving bowl. Serve immediately.

NAAN

MAKES 6 BREADS

Naan, a thick puffed flatbread, accompanies almost every Indian meal. It is traditionally baked in a tandoor, a cylindrical clay oven heated to 900°F (480°C) with a charcoal or wood fire. The dough is shaped into rounds and smacked onto the sides of the oven, where it cooks rapidly before being removed. Like pizza dough, naan blisters as it cooks. And, like homemade pizza, homemade naan is most successfully baked in a very hot oven on a stone. Since this dough is easier to manipulate and tastes better when allowed to rest, I always prepare it the day before the meal.

3 cups (420g) all-purpose flour

1 1/4 cups (300ml) lukewarm water

3/4 teaspoon quick-rising yeast

3/4 teaspoon salt

1 teaspoon sugar

1/4 cup (55g) melted butter, preferably salted, to finish

- **Prepare the dough:** In a large bowl, combine the flour, water, yeast, salt, and sugar. Using your hands, knead the mixture until it forms a soft dough. Add a little more water if it's too dry (it should not be sticky, but not too dense or dry either). Cover the bowl with a towel and let rest for 15 minutes.

- Remove the dough from the bowl and knead it on the countertop for about 5 minutes, or until a smooth, elastic ball forms. Return to the bowl, cover tightly, and let rise in a warm part of the kitchen until doubled in size, about 1 1/2 to 2 hours.

- Press the dough down gently to deflate it, then divide into 6 equal portions. Roll each piece into a ball, place the balls on a lightly floured baking sheet, cover with plastic wrap, and refrigerate. (You can prepare the dough 1 or 2 days in advance; if you do not, be sure to refrigerate it for at least a few hours before proceeding to the next step.)

- **Prepare the bread:** Remove the dough balls from the fridge about 2 hours before baking, keeping them covered. At least 30 minutes before baking, preheat the oven to 550°F (290°C) and place an oven rack in the center position. Place a baking stone on the rack (if you don't have one, you can bake the naan on an inverted baking sheet). Take 1 ball of dough, turn it out onto the counter, and press it with your fingers to stretch it. Shape into a 6-inch (15 cm) circle or oval by lifting the dough and stretching it with your hand or using a rolling pin. The dough should be quite thin.

• Place the dough on the palm of one hand, and, using your other hand, sprinkle a few drops of water over the surface. Quickly open the oven door and flip the dough over onto the hot stone. After about 1 minute, it should start to puff up. After 2 minutes, turn the bread over with tongs and bake for a further 2 minutes. Remove from the oven, place on a plate, and brush one side generously with melted butter. Keep the hot naan under a clean dish towel while you bake the rest of the bread. Serve warm.

Note: You can replace 1 cup of the all-purpose flour with whole wheat flour.

For garlic naan: Chop a clove of garlic and add it to the butter when melting it. Let it infuse for a few minutes, then either strain the garlic out or leave it in the butter before brushing it over the bread.

KULFI

Kulfi is an eggless frozen dessert often served as Popsicles.
Flavored with spices, frozen in a terrine mold, and topped with
caramelized nuts, this version is a little fancier yet still incredibly simple
to make. Serve as is or with mango slices when in season.

2 cups (500ml) whipping
cream, divided

A good pinch of saffron
threads

1 14oz (300ml) can
sweetened condensed milk

3/4 teaspoons ground
cardamom

Pistachio and Almond
Praline (recipe follows)

- Warm $1/2$ cup (125ml) cream in a saucepan, remove
  from heat, and stir in the saffron. Let cool to room
  temperature and refrigerate until well chilled.

- Line a 9 by 5 by 3-inch (23 by 12 by 7 cm) loaf pan
  with plastic wrap.

- In a large bowl, combine the chilled saffron cream and
  the remaining $1^{1}/_{2}$ cups (375ml) cream. Beat with an
  electric mixer on high speed until soft peaks form, then
  whisk in the sweetened condensed milk and cardamom
  and beat for another 10 seconds. With a rubber spatula,
  fold in the roughly chopped praline. Pour the mixture
  into the pan, cover with plastic wrap, and freeze
  overnight.

- **To serve:** Remove the plastic wrap from the top of the
  pan, dip the base of the pan in warm water, and invert
  the kulfi onto a serving dish. Remove the remaining
  plastic wrap and sprinkle with the remaining finely
  chopped praline. Slice with a hot knife, wiped clean
  between each cut, and serve immediately.

PISTACHIO AND ALMOND PRALINE

MAKES 1 ¹/₂ CUPS (ABOUT 250G)

¹/₃ cup (80ml) water

³/₄ cup (150g) sugar

¹/₂ cup (75g) almonds

¹/₄ cup (25g) pistachios

- Lightly oil a small baking sheet. Set aside.

- Pour the water into a medium saucepan and add the sugar. Bring to a boil over medium-high heat and simmer, without stirring, until the syrup turns golden. Add the nuts and stir with a wooden spoon to coat well. If the sugar crystallizes, continue stirring until it melts again.

- Transfer to the oiled baking sheet and tap against the counter so that it spreads into a thin layer. Cool completely.

- Chop two-thirds of the praline (about 1 cup) to fold into the kulfi mixture, and chop the remaining one-third (about ¹/₂ cup) a bit more finely to sprinkle over the top.

PART FIVE

Montrealers are spoiled when it comes to sweets, because both European and North American desserts are abundant here. Be it layer cake, cheesecake, mille-feuilles, cannoli, or baklava, our desserts well exemplify Montreal's style of European-meets-North-American cuisine.

As a former pastry chef trained in French baking, I tend to favor the classics, because when made with care and good ingredients, classic French desserts are hard to beat. Yet having grown up in North America, I also love a good pie, from apple to Boston cream.

Like a lot of North Americans, many Montrealers have adopted today's style of low-fat, no-carb, gluten-free, and sugar-free eating. Still—perhaps in rebellion against all that discipline—sweets are undergoing a new wave of popularity in the city thanks to a plethora of pâtisseries, bakeries, and chocolate shops and a social media scene where a picture of a cake will always "out-like" a picture of a steak.

I'm not one for daily desserts, but for a special occasion, dessert is a must at my table. For home cooks, desserts often present a challenge, as they can be more finicky to make and more time-consuming than say, a pasta or braised meat. In this chapter, I give recipes for beginners and more advanced bakers alike; just make sure to read through the recipe first. That will give you the confidence to go for it, or leave it for another time!

As for the guilt factor associated with dessert, I never feel guilty about ending the meal on a sweet note—as long as it's a high note as well.

Desserts

BERRY PAVLOVA

SERVES 6

For years, I made the same Pavlova recipe. It was good, but it often lacked the
marshmallow-textured center that makes this confection so delicious. Then I came
across pastry chef Dominique Ansel's technique, which uses a Swiss meringue base,
and the result is divine. It's quick too, taking just 30 minutes to bake. Pavlova is
traditionally garnished with passion fruit and kiwi, but as I serve this in summer,
I opt for local berries. And don't forget the powdered sugar on top to sweeten
the fruit a bit, and a sprig of mint to make it even more Instagrammable!

4 (120g) egg whites (be
sure they are fresh)

2 cups (240g) powdered
sugar, sifted

1 teaspoon vanilla

1/4 teaspoon almond extract

- Preheat the oven to 375°F (190°C). Line a baking sheet
  with parchment paper and place an 8-inch (20 cm) tart
  ring or springform pan ring on it. If you don't have a
  ring, draw an 8-inch (20 cm) circle on the parchment
  with a pencil and flip it over.

- Prepare a pot of simmering water and have ready a
  metal bowl (the one from your stand mixer, if using)
  that will fit snugly over the top of the pot without
  touching the water. Whisk the egg whites and powdered
  sugar together in the bowl, place it over the simmering
  water, and continue whisking until the mixture is just
  hot to the touch (it should read 160°F/70°C on a candy
  thermometer).

- Using a stand mixer or hand mixer, beat the whites on
  medium speed for 3 minutes. Increase the speed to high
  and beat for 2 minutes more, or until the mixture has
  cooled and tripled in volume. Transfer the meringue to
  the center of the tart (or springform) ring and, using
  the back of a spoon or a small offset spatula, spread it
  evenly into a round, then run a knife twice between the
  edges of the meringue and the ring before lifting it off.

If you aren't using a ring, spread the meringue evenly inside the drawn circle and sculpt the sides so they're smooth and high. The meringue should end up looking like a cake, not a Frisbee.

- Bake for 10 minutes, then reduce the temperature to 325°F (160°C) and bake for 20 minutes more. Remove from the oven and let cool.

- Whip the cream with the mascarpone (or crème fraîche or sour cream), sugar, and vanilla until firm peaks begin to form. Refrigerate until ready to serve.

- **Assemble the Pavlova:** Carefully transfer the Pavlova base from the baking sheet to a serving plate. Spread the cream over the top, almost to the edges. Pile on the berries. At this point, the Pavlova can be refrigerated for up to 3 hours.

- Just before serving, sprinkle with powdered sugar and garnish with mint. Serve immediately.

Topping

1 1/4 cups (310ml) whipping cream

3 tablespoons mascarpone OR crème fraîche OR sour cream

2 1/2 tablespoons sugar

1 teaspoon vanilla

About 2 cups (400g) hulled strawberries OR mixed other berries

Powdered sugar and mint sprigs to garnish

CHERRY AND BERRY CLAFOUTIS

SERVES 8

The first time I saw a clafoutis in tart form was when I was working at Montreal's
Pâtisserie de Gascogne, where we purposely used to break one every morning to
give us a chance to eat it for breakfast. This clafoutis is baked in a crust, but if crusts
make you nervous, it can also be baked directly in a ceramic or glass tart mold.

3/4lb (350g) Sweet Short-
Crust Pastry or Flaky Pie
Dough (p. 330 or p. 327)

1 teaspoon butter,
to grease the pan

Filling

2 cups (350g) fresh sour
cherries OR defrosted
frozen sour cherries OR
jarred sour cherries

1 cup (200g) blueberries
OR 1/2 cup (100g)
blueberries and 1/2 cup
(100g) raspberries

1/2 cup (125ml) milk

1/2 cup (125ml)
whipping cream

3/4 cup (150g) sugar,
divided

2 teaspoons vanilla

4 eggs

2 tablespoons
all-purpose flour

- Roll the dough out to line a lightly buttered 9 by 1^1/$_2$-
inch (23 cm by 4 cm) round tart pan (with a removable
bottom) or ceramic pie plate. Because the filling is
liquid, be sure the dough is well pressed into the corners
of the mold and free of any cracks or holes (you don't
want the filling to leak). Chill the crust until firm, at
least 1 hour.

- **Prepare the filling:** Preheat the oven to 375°F (190°C)
and place an oven rack in the lowest position in the
oven. If using fresh cherries, wash, stem, and pit them.
If using frozen or jarred, let defrost and then pat them
dry on a paper towel. Rinse the blueberries (and/or
raspberries) and set aside to dry.

- In a small saucepan, bring the milk, cream, half the
sugar, and the vanilla to a boil. Set aside. In a bowl,
whisk together the eggs with the remaining sugar, then
whisk in the flour. Pour the hot cream mixture over
the egg mixture, whisking until smooth, and strain the
mixture.

- **Assembly and baking:** Line the entire surface of the
refrigerated tart shell with parchment paper or foil
and blind-bake by filling with baking weights or beans
right to the top (this will help prevent the crust from
shrinking as it bakes). Place the tart shell on a sheet pan
and bake for about 15 to 20 minutes.

- When the shell begins to color around the sides, remove it from the oven and carefully remove the paper and weights or beans. Bake the shell for a further 5 minutes to allow the base to cook through.

- Fill the hot tart shell with the fruit, spreading it out to the edges, and pour over enough filling to reach halfway up the sides of the shell. Place it in the oven and then carefully pour in the rest of the filling so it reaches the top. Be careful not to add too much, or the filling could seep between the pastry and the tart pan.

- Bake for 10 minutes at 375°F (190°C), then reduce the heat to 350°F (175°C) and bake for about 25 to 30 minutes more. The clafoutis is cooked when the filling just begins to rise at the sides and sets in the middle. Let cool on a wire rack and unmold when warm (unless it was made in a pie pan, in which case the clafoutis should be served unmolded). Sprinkle over a pinch of granulated sugar if you like before serving.

- **For a clafoutis without a crust:** Generously butter a 9 by 1$\frac{1}{2}$-inch deep (23 by 4 cm) porcelain quiche mold or glass pie plate. Reduce the amount of cherries to 1 cup (175g) and increase the amount of flour to $\frac{1}{4}$ cup (35g).

SPOTLIGHT: MAPLE SYRUP, THE ULTIMATE QUÉBÉCOIS INGREDIENT

Like foie gras and blueberries, maple syrup is an ingredient intimately associated with Quebec. And with 11 million gallons of maple syrup produced by Quebec sugar shacks annually, accounting for more than 92 percent of all Canadian domestic production and 78 percent of the world supply, that's understandable.

With a mother from the Canadian prairies and a father from England, my syrup of choice on the breakfast table was Crown golden corn syrup. It was at cooking school that I grew to appreciate maple syrup, where it was never simply poured over pancakes, but used to make desserts like sugar tarts, maple mousse cake, maple layer cake, and maple ice cream. Unlike granulated white sugar, maple products were used not just to sweeten, but to flavor.

Today I buy light (Grade A) syrup because it has the most complex taste. Many cooks claim that the medium-grade B syrup is best for baking, but that's not always the case. "A" syrup is made from the first run of sap, which is higher in sugar (40 liters of sap to make 1 liter of syrup) than the following runs of sap, which can take up to 70 liters to make 1 liter of syrup. Because the second-run sap is less concentrated in sugar, the boiling time is longer, which is why the syrup is darker and has a more caramel-like flavor. For those of us who enjoy maple flavor with a less pronounced caramel taste, "A" syrup is the grade of choice.

In baked goods, maple syrup's delicate flavor can sometimes get lost in the shuffle. To get the most flavor from the syrup, pastry chefs often reduce it further, resulting in a strong taste of caramel. No thanks. To my mind, it's better to use maple sugar to get that rich flavor in baked goods. Made by boiling away all the water from the sap, maple sugar can be substituted for brown sugar or regular sugar in recipes from angel food cake to ice cream. And maple butter, that luscious spread that tastes like maple fudge, can also be used in recipes or simply spread generously over toasted slices of brioche or pound cake and topped with caramelized fruit.

One thing to consider is that maple is the costliest sugar in the world. Maple sugar will set you back about $20 per pound, compared to $3 for a pound of granulated white sugar. Ouch. But a little goes a long way, and you can substitute part of the maple sugar with light brown sugar and still get a pronounced maple flavor. I also like to use the larger-grained maple sugars, which can be sprinkled on puddings, cakes, cookies, cupcakes, pancakes, waffles, or ice cream.

MAPLE SUGAR TARTLETS

MAKES ABOUT 20 SMALL TARTS

These delectable tarts are a treat to serve at the end of the meal, when guests can simply pick one up and munch away. They're also lovely topped with a cloud of whipped cream, and if you want to go full-on Québécois, add a few blueberries.

1 1/3 cups (165g) maple sugar

1/3 cup (65g) packed brown sugar

2 1/2 tablespoons all-purpose flour

Pinch of salt

1 large egg

1/4 cup (60ml) milk

3/4 cup (180ml) whipping cream

1 recipe Sweet Short-Crust Pastry (p. 330)

Whipped cream to serve (optional)

- In a medium bowl, mix the maple sugar, brown sugar, flour, and salt together. Lightly whisk together the egg and milk, and fold into the sugar mixture, without overmixing. Gently stir in the cream with a spatula and let the mixture stand for at least an hour on the counter (or in the fridge, if longer than an hour), stirring occasionally.

- Have at the ready a standard, 12-cup muffin tin and 12 mini muffin liners, as well as baking weights or dried beans.

- On a lightly floured surface, roll out the dough to 1/4-inch-thick (about 1/2 cm) and cut out 20, 3- to 4-inch (7 to 10 cm) rounds. Line the muffin cups with 12 of the rounds (reserve the rest in the fridge), pressing the dough well into the sides of each. Place a paper muffin liner in each tart shell and fill halfway with the baking weights. Refrigerate while you preheat your oven to 350°F (180°C).

- Bake the shells for 20 minutes, then remove the baking weights and papers and return to the oven for another 3 minutes. You can then unmold the baked tart shells onto another parchment-lined tray, and repeat the process with the reserved dough rounds to make about 20 shells in all.

- When all the shells are ready, fill each tart shell with about 3 tablespoons of the maple sugar mixture. Aim to get the mixture right to the rim. Carefully place them back in the oven and immediately lower the temperature to 325°F (160°C). Bake for about 15 minutes, or until the filling begins to rise and bubble a little. The filling should be set when you jiggle the pan. Let cool completely before serving.

MAPLE PECAN PIE

This pecan pie is rich but not over the top and makes a fine sugar pie if you
leave out the nuts. Walnuts are also great in place of the pecans, though
in either case, it's essential to find the best-quality nuts available.

1 9-inch (23 cm) unbaked
tart shell made with Sweet
Short-Crust Pastry or
Flaky Pie Dough (p. 330 or
p. 327)

5 egg yolks

1 egg

2/3 cup (160ml) maple syrup

1 cup (210g) packed brown
sugar

1/2 cup (110g) butter,
melted

1/2 cup (125ml)
whipping cream

Pinch of salt

1 tablespoon all-purpose
flour

1 1/2 cups (160g) pecans

- Prepare a pot of simmering water that can hold a metal
  bowl snugly without the bowl touching the water. In
  the bowl, vigorously whisk together the egg yolks, egg,
  maple syrup, brown sugar, butter, cream, salt, and flour.
  Set over the water bath and cook, stirring often, until
  the mixture thickens enough to coat the back of a spoon
  (185°F/85°C on a candy thermometer).

- When the mixture is the right consistency, remove
  from the heat and strain into a blender container or
  tall measuring cup. Then, using the blender or a hand
  blender, blend the mixture at high speed for 1 minute.
  Place in the refrigerator to chill thoroughly. Overnight is
  ideal, but a few hours should suffice.

- Preheat your oven to 350°F (180°C). Place the nuts on a
  cookie sheet and toast them until they begin to release
  their aroma. Remove from the oven and set aside.
  Increase the oven temperature to 400°F (200°C).

- **Assemble the tart:** Now you can either place the nuts in
  the bottom of the shell and pour over the sugar mixture,
  or pour the mixture into the shell and arrange the nuts
  on top.

- Bake the pie for about 10 minutes, then reduce the
  temperature to 275°F (135°C) and bake for 30 minutes,
  or until the filling is set in the middle. It shouldn't
  jiggle, but the filling shouldn't rise either. Let cool
  completely on a rack, then serve at room temperature.

APPLE GALETTE

SERVES 6 TO 8

This style of free-form tart is ideal for those who find rolling dough a challenge. These even look better when they're a bit on the rustic side. I like to serve this galette with ice cream—vanilla works, of course, but the caramel ice cream recipe that follows is my favorite with apple pie. It's also delicious with a slice of Cheddar cheese.

¾lb (350g) Flaky Pie Dough (p. 327)

4 baking apples (Golden, Cortland, Pink Lady, Honeycrisp, Granny Smith, etc.)

⅓ cup (70g) packed brown sugar

1 tablespoon cornstarch

Pinch of salt

1 teaspoon freshly grated lemon zest

½ teaspoon ground cinnamon

1 egg, beaten

1 tablespoon sugar

1 tablespoon cold butter, cut into pieces

- Preheat the oven to 400°F (200°C). Prepare a parchment-lined baking sheet.

- On a lightly floured countertop, roll out the dough into a 14-inch (35 cm) circle. Transfer the dough to the baking sheet and refrigerate.

- Peel and core the apples, then thinly slice.

- In a large bowl, combine the brown sugar, cornstarch, salt, lemon zest, and cinnamon. Add the apple slices and toss (with your hands, preferably) to coat well with the sugar mixture.

- Mound the apples in the center of the circle of dough and, leaving about a 2-inch (5 cm) border all around, pat them into an even layer. (If you have the time, you can arrange them in concentric circles.) Fold the edges of the dough over to partially enclose the apples, pleating the dough to fit, then lightly press down on the pleats to keep the crust from rising when baking. Brush the edges of the pastry with the beaten egg and sprinkle lightly with the granulated sugar. Place the butter pieces on top of the apples.

- Bake until the filling begins to bubble and the crust is golden brown, about 45 minutes. Don't worry if the juices escape a little, it won't show when it's done.

- Remove the tart from the oven and cool slightly on a wire rack. Transfer to a serving plate and serve warm or at room temperature.

**Strawberry/Rhubarb
Variation:**

⅓ cup (65g) sugar

1 teaspoon grated
orange zest

2 tablespoons cornstarch

Pinch of salt

1lb (450g) rhubarb, washed,
trimmed, and cut into 1-inch
(2.5 cm) pieces

1 cup (170g) sliced
strawberries

- Follow the same procedure as for the apple galette, but for the filling: In a large bowl, rub together the sugar and zest, then add the cornstarch and salt. Add the rhubarb and strawberries and toss (with your hands, preferably) to coat well with sugar.

CARAMEL ICE CREAM

MAKES 4 CUPS (1 L)

This ice cream is the perfect match for the Apple Galette (p. 276), though you could serve it alone, or even with the Perfect Little Chocolate Cake (p. 285).

¾ cup (150g) +
2 tablespoons sugar

2 tablespoons light
corn syrup

Pinch of salt

3 tablespoons water

1 tablespoon butter

2 cups (500ml) milk

6 egg yolks

- Rinse out a medium thick-bottomed pot, but don't dry it; then add the ¾ cup sugar and the corn syrup. Place over medium-high heat and stir just to combine, then allow to bubble away, untouched.

- When the sugar is fully melted and begins to color around the edges, start to lightly swirl the syrup as it bubbles away until it becomes an even golden brown, about 4 minutes. Now watch the mixture carefully. As soon as the caramel releases a first burst of smoke, turn off the heat and whisk in the water, followed by the

⟶

(continued)

butter and salt. Remove from the heat and strain into a small bowl. Cover and set aside to cool to room temperature. Don't bother cleaning the pot; you'll need it for the next step.

- Have ready a large bowl of ice water, a fine strainer, and a smaller bowl which you can place in the ice bath to chill, as well as a wooden spoon and, if using, a candy thermometer.

- Pour the milk into the saucepan you used to make the caramel and set it over high heat. Heat, whisking on occasion, until it comes to a boil.

- Meanwhile, whisk the 2 tablespoons of sugar with the egg yolks in a bowl until the mixture has a creamy consistency. Slowly whisk half the scalded milk into the egg mixture, lower the heat to medium, and whisk the egg mixture back into the pot of milk. Using the wooden spoon, stir the mixture until it's thick enough to coat the back of the spoon and leaves a trace when your finger is drawn through it, or until it reaches 185°F (85°C) on the candy thermometer. Remove from the heat and immediately whisk in the cooled caramel, then strain the mixture into the chilled bowl. Chill thoroughly over the ice bath and then refrigerate (overnight is ideal).

- Churn the mixture in an ice cream machine following manufacturer's instructions. Place a container in the freezer to chill while the ice cream churns, then transfer the ice cream into the frozen container and freeze until ready to serve.

Cakes Small and Large

CAROLINE'S POUDING CHÔMEUR

Easily one of the most famous recipes in Quebec, the pudding cake known as pouding chômeur (unemployment pudding) is credited to Georgette Falardeau, wife of member of parliament and four-time mayor of Montreal, Camilien Houde. Mme Falardeau created this inexpensive dessert, consisting of a basic white cake baked in a brown sugar sauce, during the Depression, and a later version was popularized by Quebec culinary icon Jehane Benoît. Eventually most every Québécois family had its own version of this dessert. However, to me there is but one seriously delicious take on this Quebec classic, and that is the recipe by Montreal chef Caroline Dumas. The secret of Dumas's recipe, which she credits to her grandmother, a native of the maple-rich region of the Beauce, is that the traditional brown sugar sauce is replaced with one made with cream and maple syrup. Though some classic versions call for the addition of maple syrup to the sauce, the cream/maple syrup idea is Dumas's, resulting in a cake that's posh enough to have been on the menu at Martin Picard's restaurant Au Pied de Cochon since its opening in 2002. You can serve it solo, but I like to follow Picard's lead and top it with a scoop of vanilla ice cream. Major yum!

2 cups (500ml) maple syrup

2 cups (500ml) whipping cream

2 cups minus 2 tablespoons (265g) all-purpose flour

2 teaspoons baking powder

1/4 teaspoon salt

1/2 cup (110g) butter, at room temperature

1/2 cup (100g) sugar

2 eggs

1/2 cup (125ml) milk

- Preheat the oven to 375° F (190°C) and have ready a 9 by 13-inch (23 by 20 cm) baking pan. No need to grease it.

- In a deep pot, bring the maple syrup and cream to a boil. Be careful, it rises up quickly! Reduce the heat to medium-low and simmer for about 5 minutes to reduce the syrup a bit. Remove from the heat and set aside.

- In a small bowl, combine the flour, baking powder, and salt. In the bowl of a stand mixer with the paddle attachment, or in a medium bowl using an electric hand mixer, cream together the butter and sugar at high speed, then beat in the eggs one at a time. Reduce the mixer speed to low and add the dry ingredients alternately with the milk, beating until smooth.

→

- Spread the batter in the pan. At this point, you can proceed with the recipe or refrigerate the batter in the pan and bake it 30 minutes before you intend to serve the cake.

- When ready to bake: Set aside about ⅓ cup (75ml) of sauce to pour over the cake when serving, and pour the rest over the batter to fill the pan two-thirds full. Bake until the cake is firm and golden on top, about 30 minutes. Serve warm with the extra sauce poured over the top of each portion, with or without a scoop of vanilla ice cream.

THE PERFECT LITTLE CHOCOLATE CAKE

This single-layer cake, inspired by a recipe from French baker Jean-Luc
Poujauran, looks unassuming, but it hits all of my chocolate cake
requirements. It's full-flavored without being overly rich, though I've
added an icing to make it even more irresistible.

6 tablespoons (82g) butter

1 teaspoon vanilla

½ teaspoon instant
espresso powder

½ cup + 3 tablespoons
(90g) pastry flour

1 teaspoon baking powder

¼ cup (30g) cocoa powder

3 eggs

½ cup + 2 tablespoons
(120g) sugar

Pinch of salt

¼ cup (60ml) whipping
cream

→

- Grease an 8-inch (20 cm) round or square cake pan and
  line the base with parchment paper.

- Melt the butter with the vanilla and espresso powder
  and set aside. Sift together the flour, baking powder,
  and cocoa powder and set aside as well.

- In the bowl of a stand mixer fitted with the whisk
  attachment, or in a large bowl using an electric hand
  mixer, beat the eggs with the sugar and salt at medium-
  high speed until doubled in volume. Gently stir in the
  dry ingredients, then fold in the butter alternately with
  the cream. Pour into the cake pan and spread evenly
  right into the corners. Chill for 30 minutes.

- Meanwhile, heat the oven to 350°F (180°C). Bake the
  cake for 25 minutes. Cool and unmold. Transfer to a
  serving plate, remove the parchment, and ice the top
  and sides generously in a swirling motion.

→

(continued)

Icing

2oz (60g) semisweet
chocolate, chopped

1/3 cup (80ml) whipping
cream, divided

3 tablespoons (40g) butter,
at room temperature

2 tablespoons sifted
powdered sugar (optional)*

Pinch of salt

- Place the chocolate in a medium bowl.

- In a small saucepan, bring the cream to a boil. Remove from the heat and pour half the cream over the chocolate. Whisk until shiny and smooth and then gradually blend in the rest of the cream. Let cool to room temperature. When the cream mixture is completely cool, using a hand mixer at high speed, beat in the butter, a tablespoon at a time, then the powdered sugar and salt. Continue beating until the icing holds a peak when the beater is lifted.

*Note: If you prefer a less-sweet icing, leave out the powdered sugar.

BANANA CAKE

My inspiration for this recipe was the Sara Lee banana cakes of my youth, but because it's homemade, it's even better. It goes without saying that for the best banana flavor, be sure to use overripe bananas. I frost it with a cream cheese icing, but it's also nice left plain.

2 cups (280g) all-purpose flour

1 teaspoon baking soda

1 teaspoon baking powder

1 teaspoon salt

1 1/2 cups (300g) sugar

3 eggs, separated

1/2 cup (125ml) vegetable oil

1 cup (250ml) mashed banana (about 3 medium bananas)

1/2 cup (125ml) buttermilk

Cream Cheese Icing

6 tablespoons (80g) cream cheese, at room temperature

6 tablespoons (80g) butter, at room temperature

2 cups (250g) powdered sugar, sifted

1 teaspoon vanilla

1 tablespoon lemon juice or rum

- Preheat the oven to 350°F (175°C). Grease a 9 by 13-inch (23 by 33 cm) baking pan, then line the base with parchment paper.

- Sift together the flour, baking soda, baking powder, and salt. Set 2 large spoonfuls of the sugar aside.

- In the bowl of a stand mixer fitted with the whisk attachment or in a large bowl using a hand mixer, beat the egg yolks at high speed with half the remaining sugar, then slowly incorporate the oil. Add the remaining sugar and beat until light in texture, then add the mashed banana and buttermilk and mix well. Add the dry ingredients to the banana mixture and blend until smooth.

- In a medium-sized, immaculately clean glass or stainless steel bowl, using a hand mixer or with a whisk, beat the egg whites with the reserved 2 spoonfuls of sugar until they hold soft peaks. Don't overwhip them, or the cake will rise and then fall. Fold the whites into the base mixture until blended.

- Spread the batter evenly in the prepared cake pan and bake for 40 to 45 minutes, or until a toothpick inserted in the center of the cake comes out clean. Let cool in the pan, then frost with the cream cheese icing.

- **For the icing:** Beat together the cream cheese, butter, powdered sugar, vanilla, and lemon juice (or rum) until smooth and spreadable.

BOSTON CREAM PIE

SERVES 8 TO 10

This simple cake, known in my house as the "Mae West de Luxe," is equally popular with French and English Canadians. It also seems to be the cake of choice for every grandparent's birthday. To alleviate its often-dry texture, I cut the cake into thirds to create two layers of custard that I lighten with a bit of cream, but feel free to stick to a single layer of custard, if you like.

Sponge Cake

MAKES 1 8-INCH (20 CM) OR 9-INCH (23 CM) CAKE

1 1/2 cups (170g) pastry flour

1/2 teaspoon baking powder

1/4 teaspoon baking soda

Pinch of salt

1/2 cup (110g) butter, at room temperature

1 tablespoon vegetable oil

3/4 cup + 2 tablespoons (175g) sugar

2 eggs, at room temperature

1 teaspoon vanilla

2/3 cup (160ml) buttermilk

- Preheat the oven to 350°F (180°C). Line the bottom of an 8-inch (20 cm) or 9-inch (23 cm) cake pan with parchment paper. No need to grease the sides of the pan.

- Sift together the flour, baking powder, baking soda, and salt.

- In the bowl of a stand mixer or a large bowl using a hand mixer, cream together the butter, oil, and sugar at high speed until fluffy. Scrape down the sides of the bowl, then add the eggs one at a time and the vanilla and continue beating until light and well blended.

- On low speed, add the dry ingredients, alternating with the buttermilk, about one-third of each at a time. Scrape down the bowl one last time and give it a final stir until you have a smooth batter.

- Pour the batter into the prepared pan, spread it to even out the surface, and bake for 40 to 45 minutes, or until the cake is golden brown and bounces back easily when pressed.

- Cool for 10 minutes on a wire rack, then run a spatula or knife between the cake and the sides of the pan to loosen it, and unmold. Cool completely before slicing.

- This cake can be made ahead and stored, well wrapped, in the fridge or freezer until ready to use.

Custard Filling

MAKES 2 CUPS (500ML)

1 cup (250ml) milk

1 teaspoon vanilla (or
the pulp from a split and
scraped vanilla bean)

⅓ cup (70g) sugar, divided

3 egg yolks

2 tablespoons cornstarch

2 tablespoons butter

½ cup (125ml)
whipping cream

⟶

- In a medium saucepan, combine the milk, vanilla, and half the sugar and bring to a boil.

- Meanwhile, in a small bowl, vigorously whisk the egg yolks and remaining sugar until smooth and pale. Add the cornstarch and continue whisking until smooth.

- Pour half the hot milk into the egg mixture. Whisk until smooth, then pour it back into the pan of hot milk. Still whisking, bring back to a boil and boil for about 15 seconds, until the custard is smooth and thick. Remove from the heat and whisk in the butter. Transfer to a clean bowl and cover with plastic wrap pressed against the surface of the custard. Refrigerate immediately. The custard will keep for 5 days in the fridge.

- **To finish the filling:** In a small bowl, whip the cream until stiff peaks form. In a larger bowl, whip the custard vigorously until it's smooth and lump-free. Whisk a large spoonful of the whipped cream into the custard, then fold in the rest with a spatula.

- **To assemble the cake:** Place the sponge cake on your serving plate so that the bottom crust is on top, and peel off the parchment paper. Cut the cake horizontally in half, spread the cream evenly over the bottom layer, going right up to the edges, and cover it with the other half of the sponge cake. (Or, cut the cake horizontally into thirds and spread half the cream on the bottom layer. Top with the second layer, spread the rest of the cream on top, and top with the final layer.) Refrigerate while you make the glaze.

⟶

(continued)

Ganache Glaze

¼ cup (60ml)
whipping cream

1 tablespoon corn syrup

2oz (55g) bittersweet
chocolate, chopped

1 tablespoon butter,
at room temperature

⅓ cup (40g) powdered
sugar, sifted

- In a small saucepan, bring the cream and corn syrup to a boil. Off the heat, add the chocolate. Count to 30, then whisk it all together to obtain a smooth texture. Add the butter and then the powdered sugar and whisk again until smooth and glossy.

- Pour the warm chocolate glaze over the cake and spread evenly over the top, allowing it to run down the sides. Refrigerate the cake until ready to serve.

Tea à la Montrealaise

Tea is as English as the Royals, the Beatles, Harry Potter, and fish and chips. My earliest childhood memories include staring down into a mug of milky tea before school. And the first time I ever drank alcohol was a small glass of sherry at a tea offered by my Scottish neighbors. Thanks to my English/Irish heritage, afternoon tea has been a longstanding favorite, not to mention the ideal opportunity to enjoy yet another slice of cake.

I always figured one of the factors that differenciated the French and English communities in my city, besides the language, was our preference for tea over coffee. Not so. Tea is a big deal in Montreal. No longer the Anglo beverage of choice, a cup of fine tea is an olfactory experience for anyone interested in discovering beautiful flavors.

Montrealers have access to some of the best tea in North America, and there are also several excellent salons de thé (tea rooms) in the city. I've enjoyed a cuppa at both the Ritz-Carlton and the Queen Elizabeth hotels, where afternoon tea is not an old-fashioned tradition, but a shorter, less costly, and far less boozy version of the power lunch.

Having attended some serious tea tastings in Montreal, I can attest that there are more Francophiles than Anglophiles in the room. At Montreal's top tea shop, Camellia Senensis, 80 percent of the clients are French-speaking. Co-owner Kevin Gascoyne confirms that the Francophile lust for tea is burgeoning. "I think the popularity of high-end tea follows the new curiosity for the exotic," he says. "That French legacy of 'degustation' and discovery is very strong here."

Tips for perfect tea

Tea, too often prepared by adding a bag to the teapot, is sometimes more of a routine than a real pleasure. It's a shame to set the bar so low for an ingredient that can reach such heights. Brewed correctly, loose-leaf teas can give off a floral fragrance or a muscatel taste, as well as offering a lovely texture, body, and a nutty finish. Here are a few suggestions for preparing a top-notch cup of tea.

— I love Earl Grey, but purists, who sometimes find the flavors of fragrant tea overwhelming, opt for tea leaves ranging from white to black (the color of tea is not a question of variety but of fermentation) rather than blends, flavored teas, and herbs for infusion. To fully appreciate the greatness of tea, try the original varieties and look for a batch number on the label.

— To take tasting to the next level, always choose fresh tea, keeping in mind that harvest periods will vary from region to region. For example, for Darjeeling teas, the new tea (first flush) arrives in spring, and second flush at the end of July.

— Always heat your teapot before brewing. You can do this by filling it with boiling water and emptying it when it's hot to the touch. Add the tea, then add fresh water that has had time to reach the desired temperature (see below).

— Infusion requires precision. Count 1 generous teaspoon of tea leaves per cup (2$\frac{1}{2}$g, to be precise). The water temperature should be 203°F (95°C) for black teas, 185°F (85°C) for white teas, and 176°F (80°C) for green teas. Infusion time will range between 3 and 5 minutes, depending on the type of tea.

— Tea can be expensive, but quality leaves can be infused up to 3 times.

— Enjoy your tea. If you're doing a home tasting, use two teapots and brew two teas side by side to compare them. The range of subtle and diverse flavors will be astonishing. Green teas offer fresh, fruity, and floral notes. More oxidized teas, such as black teas, tend to be robust and astringent. As tea cools, its flavors become more pronounced. If you can get your hands on a rare and delicious white tea, you'll notice that its taste is subtle when hot but develops at room temperature.

— As for milk, sugar, or lemon, it's up to you, but purists would say these flavor enhancers are just distractions.

Tea Cakes & Cookies

There's a lull between meals in the late afternoon that's perfect for a cup of tea and a slice of cake. What I like about tea cakes is that they last for days on the kitchen counter and are ideal for adding to boxed lunches or handing to the kids—or yourself!—as a 4 o'clock snack. These cakes are simple to make, so why not make two, wrap one up, and offer it as a gift? I also love small cakes served with fruit and cheese at a dinner party. A bowl of tangerines or strawberries with a plate of financiers or madeleines is the perfect way to end a meal. And if it's not cake that ends up on my plate, it's cookies—which, in my house, disappear almost instantly after coming out of the oven.

FINANCIERS

MAKES 20 MINI CAKES

Like madeleines, these dense little almond cakes are crisp on the outside and melting within, so eat them the day they are made to enjoy them at their best. Financiers are traditionally baked in rectangular molds shaped like gold bars (from which their name is derived), but I prefer using mini muffin tins, which are easier to find.

½ cup (110g) butter

½ cup (60g) almond flour

1 cup (120g) powdered sugar, sifted

3 egg whites (90g), lightly whisked

½ cup (70g) all-purpose flour

1 teaspoon vanilla

1 teaspoon rum

Pinch of salt

Butter and flour for preparing the pans

- Brown the butter (see instructions on p. 326); strain and set aside.

- In a medium bowl, combine the almond flour and powdered sugar. Stir in half the whites to make a thick batter, then gradually blend in the rest. Stir in the flour until just combined, followed by the vanilla, rum, salt, and brown butter, stirring until you end up with a velvety batter. Cover and refrigerate for an hour.

- Preheat the oven to 425°F (210°C). Butter and flour financier molds or a mini muffin pan and fill the cups halfway with the batter. Bake for 10 to 12 minutes, until the cakes are golden. Repeat the process to use up all the batter.

- Unmold when still warm and serve immediately or at room temperature. They are best eaten the same day, but you can store any leftovers well wrapped.

MAPLE SUGAR MADELEINES

MAKES 16 LARGE MADELEINES

These famous French cakes are a treat any time of day. I make mine with maple sugar and add the pulp from a vanilla bean if I have one handy. The beauty of madeleines is that the batter keeps very well in the fridge, so you can bake only the number you plan to eat that day.

2 eggs

2/3 cup (85g) maple sugar

1 tablespoon brown sugar

1 tablespoon maple syrup

1/2 teaspoon vanilla

Pinch of salt

2/3 cup (90g) all-purpose flour

1 teaspoon baking powder

6 tablespoons (80g) butter, melted and cooled

About 2 tablespoons melted butter for greasing the pan

- In a medium bowl with an electric mixer, or by hand with a whisk, beat the eggs with the sugars and syrup until creamy. Blend in the vanilla and salt and then gently stir in the flour and baking powder. Add the 6 tablespoons (80g) melted butter and stir to form a smooth batter. Cover and refrigerate for a few hours or, better yet, overnight.

- Preheat the oven to 425°F (210°C). Generously butter your madeleine pan with the 2 tablespoons of melted butter.

- Using two spoons or a piping bag, fill the molds three-quarters full to get 16 madeleines. Bake for 3 minutes, then reduce the heat to 400°F (200°C) and bake for 7 minutes more, or until the madeleines are deep golden brown. Let cool and serve the day they are made.

ORANGE ALMOND CAKE

SERVES 8

As much as I love all lemon tea cakes, once I tried this one with almond and orange, it became my favorite. It's incredibly simple to make, but don't leave out the glaze, because it makes all the difference.

9 tablespoons (125g) butter, at room temperature

1 1/2 cups (180g) powdered sugar

1 tablespoon finely grated orange zest

4 eggs

3/4 cup (90g) pastry flour

1 1/4 cups (125g) almond flour

1/2 teaspoon baking powder

Glaze

2/3 cup (85g) powdered sugar, sifted

2 tablespoons freshly squeezed orange juice or passion fruit juice

- Preheat the oven to 375°F (190 °C). Butter and flour a 9 by 5 by 3-inch (23 by 12 by 7 cm) loaf pan.

- In the bowl of a stand mixer fitted with the paddle attachment, or in a large bowl with an electric mixer, beat the butter with the powdered sugar and orange zest until light and very creamy. Add the eggs one at a time, making sure each is well incorporated before adding the next.

- Beat in the flour, almond flour, and baking powder until smooth and then pour the batter into the pan. Bake for 40 to 50 minutes, or until a cake tester comes out clean. Let cool slightly on a rack and unmold when warm.

- **For the glaze:** In a small bowl, whisk the powdered sugar and juice together and then, using a pastry brush, brush the glaze all over the top and sides of the warm cake. Let cool completely on a rack before slicing.

COCONUT CAKE

This cake is rich and buttery, and yet the texture is so light that I guarantee you'll be reaching for a second piece before you finish the first. The amount of coconut is just right, but don't be tempted to use all-purpose flour here, or the cake will be too heavy.

1¾ cups (190g) butter

1¾ cups (245g) pastry flour

½ teaspoon baking powder

½ teaspoon salt

⅔ cup (60g) flaked coconut

4 eggs

1 cup (200g) sugar

1 teaspoon finely grated lime zest

¼ teaspoon coconut or almond extract

1 teaspoon vanilla

¼ cup (25g) slivered almonds

Sifted powdered sugar to finish (optional)

- Preheat the oven to 350°F (180°C). Butter a 9-inch (23 cm) round cake pan or springform pan and line the bottom with a round of parchment paper.

- Melt the butter and set aside to cool. Sift together the flour, baking powder, and salt into a bowl, then stir in the coconut.

- In a large bowl, beat the eggs with the sugar and lime zest until doubled in volume. Add the dry ingredients all at once and mix until smooth. Gradually pour in the butter, along with the extracts, and blend until smooth. Pour the batter into the prepared pan and sprinkle over the slivered almonds.

- Bake for 40 minutes, or until the top of the cake is light golden and it begins to pull away from the sides. Let cool completely before serving, dusted with a bit of powdered sugar, if you like.

ROSITA'S COOKIES

MAKES 32 COOKIES

This recipe was inspired by cookies that were sold at a bakery in my neighborhood
in my childhood called Graham Pastry, which everyone referred to as Rosita's, after the
wonderful saleslady in charge. The bakery is now long gone, and the original recipe, alas,
died with its maker. But a baker friend of mine, André Perron, sent me this recipe
to compare, and it's pretty darn close. You will need a piping bag and two kinds of flour
to make them, but the resulting sablés are so elegant and delicious that they are
worth the extra trouble. These cookies can be eaten as is or sandwiched
with jam or caramel sauce, or dipped in tempered chocolate.

½ cup + 1 tablespoon (125g) butter, at room temperature

¾ cup + 1 tablespoon (110g) powdered sugar, sifted

Pinch of salt

⅓ cup (35g) pastry flour, sifted

1 cup (140g) bread flour

3 tablespoons (45ml) hot milk

1 teaspoon vanilla

- Preheat your oven to 375°F (190°C). Prepare two cookie sheets lined with parchment paper.

- In the bowl of a stand mixer fitted with the paddle attachment or in a large bowl with an electric mixer, beat the butter on high speed until very soft and creamy. Add the powdered sugar and salt, and continue beating until smooth. In a small bowl, combine the two flours, then add half of the mix to the butter mixture and beat on medium speed until just combined; add the rest alternately with the hot milk and vanilla. Mix again just until you have a smooth, soft dough.

- Using a piping bag with a star tip, pipe the cookies into swirls, rosettes, or batonnets onto the parchment paper, spacing them about 2 inches (5 cm) apart. Bake for 15 to 17 minutes, until deep golden. Do not undercook them, or they will taste floury.

- **Variation:** I also make a butterscotch version of these cookies, substituting ½ cup (110g) packed brown sugar for the powdered sugar and piping the cookies in round swirls.

PART SIX

Base Recipes

Clarified Butter

Place the butter in a small saucepan and melt slowly. As the butter melts the milk solids will drop to the bottom and a foam will form on top. Skim off the foam and slowly pass the butter through a fine sieve (or cheesecloth) to remove the milk solids, which can be discarded.

Brown Butter

In a small deep saucepan, melt the butter over medium-low heat (you'll need to be on the lookout for the next steps to ensure that the butter caramelizes properly). After a good 5 minutes, the milk solids will have dropped to the bottom and a foam will form on the surface. Once the butter begins to color (and the foam diminishes considerably), move the foam to the side of the pan to keep an eye on the color. When it has turned a beautiful shade of amber, remove the pan from the heat. Allow to cool, then strain the liquid through a fine sieve (or cheesecloth) to remove the caramelized milk solids, which can be discarded.

FLAKY PIE DOUGH (PÂTE BRISÉE)

MAKES ENOUGH DOUGH FOR A SINGLE 9-INCH (23 CM) PIECRUST

This multipurpose dough can be used for both sweet and savory pies; just leave out the sugar if you are making a savory pie. The vinegar helps keep the dough from oxidizing but you can omit it, if desired. I've added a second method here for using a food processor.

1 ⅓ cups (185g) all-purpose flour

2 teaspoons sugar

¼ teaspoon salt

⅓ cup (75g) cold unsalted butter, cut into small cubes

3 tablespoons (45g) cold shortening, cut into small cubes

¼ cup (60 ml) ice water

¼ teaspoon white vinegar (optional)

- Place the flour in a large bowl, or directly on the counter and stir in the sugar and salt. Add the butter and shortening and toss to coat with the flour.

- Using your fingers or a pastry blender, break up the butter and shortening, at first pinching them, then breaking them further into pea-sized pieces in the flour, trying your best not to squish the butter right into the flour. You can stop when most of the fat is broken up, as it doesn't matter if you have a few larger pieces in the mix. Make a well in the center of the flour, then pour in the ice water and vinegar (if using). Using your fingers, slowly incorporate the liquid into the flour mixture until a dough begins to form. If the dough seems dry, you can add another tablespoon of water, but add it a little at a time; it's preferable if your dough is just a bit crumbly and in no way sticky.

- Knead the dough on the counter by pushing it away from you using the heel of your hand until it is smooth, 4 or 5 times; avoiding overworking it, or it will become tough. Ideally, you will still see small bits of butter in the dough. Shape the dough into a flat disk, tucking under the edges to make it smooth, as this will facilitate rolling later. Wrap the dough in plastic wrap and refrigerate until ready to use. This dough must be chilled thoroughly, for at least a few hours, before rolling, or, ideally, overnight.

⟶

(continued)

Food processor method:

- Place the flour, sugar, and salt in a bowl and toss in the cubes of butter and lard. Place in the freezer for 30 minutes.

- Transfer the mixture to the bowl of your food processor, fitted with the chopping blade, and pulse for 2 seconds to break up the fat into the flour. Repeat about 3 times, or until the fat is in small pieces. Do not overmix.

- Combine the water and vinegar and, with the machine running, pour it through the feed tube. Pulse until the dough begins to clump together. It will still be crumbly.

- Knead the dough on the counter by pushing it away from you using the heel of your hand until it is smooth, 4 or 5 times; avoiding overworking it, or it will become tough. If it is still crumbly, add 1 to 2 tablespoons more water. Ideally, you will still see a few small pieces of butter in the dough.

- Wrap in plastic wrap and refrigerate for at least 1 hour before using. The dough should be chilled completely, preferably overnight, before rolling.

LARD-AND-BUTTER PASTRY

MAKES ENOUGH DOUGH FOR A DOUBLE 9-INCH (23 CM) PIECRUST

2⅔ cups (375g) all-purpose flour

Pinch of sugar

¾ teaspoon salt

⅔ cup (150g) cold unsalted butter, cut into small cubes

6 tbsp (90g) cold lard, cut into small cubes

½ cup (120ml) ice water

1 teaspoon white vinegar

- Use the same method as for the Flaky Pie Dough (p. 327) or the food processor method. When the dough is ready, divide it in half and flatten each piece into a disk.

- Wrap in plastic wrap and refrigerate for at least 1 hour before using. The dough should be chilled completely, preferably overnight, before rolling.

SWEET SHORT-CRUST PASTRY (PÂTE SUCRÉE)

MAKES ENOUGH DOUGH FOR A SINGLE 9-INCH (23 CM) PIECRUST

½ cup (110g) unsalted butter, at room temperature

⅓ cup (40g) powdered sugar, sifted

Pinch of salt

2 egg yolks

1 tablespoon ice water

1¼ cups (175g) all-purpose flour

- With an electric mixer or by hand, in a medium bowl, beat the butter, powdered sugar, and salt until smooth and creamy. Blend in the egg yolks one by one, followed by the water. Stir in the flour until you have a ragged dough, then turn it out onto a lightly floured counter and knead it gently until it has a uniform consistency, without overworking it. Flatten into a disk, wrap in plastic wrap, and refrigerate for at least 2 hours before rolling (or 4 hours before grating).

- To roll out the dough: Remove the dough from the refrigerator, cut it into large pieces, and, working quickly, press it between your hands, like Play-Doh, to soften. Press them together into a ball and flatten into a disk, tucking under the edges to make them smooth. You want your dough to be malleable but still cool.

- On a lightly floured surface, roll the dough out into a large round (about 13 inches/33 cm), keeping the counter and dough floured at all times and rotating the dough a quarter of a turn every few rolls. Continue rolling out the dough until it reaches a ⅛-inch thickness (2 to 3 mm), or until you just begin to see the pattern of your counter through the dough. Give the dough a final turn, flour it lightly, and carefully roll it up around the rolling pin, then unroll it into a 9-inch (23 cm) tart pan with a removable bottom.

- Carefully press the dough into the pan, being sure to get it right into the corners and trying to make the sides as high as possible so they won't sink down when baking. Trim off any excess, overhanging dough. If you end up with any holes or cracks, use the dough trimmings to patch it together. Make sure the top rim of the tart isn't too thin. Chill for about 30 minutes before baking. Keep any leftover dough refrigerated; it can be incorporated into fresh dough for your next crust.

If rolling out dough makes you nervous, try this technique.

- To use the grating method: Once the dough is very cold, grate it on the medium holes of a box grater. Scatter half the grated dough around the edges of a 9-inch (23 cm) tart pan with a removable bottom, and press the dough evenly against the sides and well into the corners. Then press the remaining dough evenly over the base, making sure the entire surface of the pan is evenly covered by about a $1/8$-inch (3 mm) thickness of dough and that there aren't any holes. Chill the tart base until firm, at least 30 minutes, before baking.

CLASSIC TOMATO SAUCE

MAKES ABOUT 6 CUPS (1.5 LITERS)

1 34oz (796ml) can plum tomatoes, ideally San Marzano, with their juices

About 1/3 cup (80ml) olive oil

1 medium onion, chopped

4 large garlic cloves, smashed and peeled but left whole

2 tablespoons tomato paste

1 22oz (660ml) jar tomato purée (passata)

2 teaspoons salt

Freshly ground black pepper

Handful of fresh basil leaves

- Pour the plum tomatoes, with their juices, into a small bowl and crush with your hands or a potato masher.

- In a large thick-bottomed pot or Dutch oven, heat the oil over medium-high heat. Add the onions and sauté until they're soft, then add the garlic. Stir in the tomato paste and cook for a minute more.

- Carefully pour in the passata and crushed tomatoes, being careful that the oil doesn't bubble up and splatter. Fill the passata jar halfway with water, cover, shake, and pour the water into the sauce as well. Stir the sauce, season with the salt and a little pepper, reduce the heat to medium-low, and simmer until it reaches the consistency of porridge (it should reduce by about a third).

- Remove the garlic cloves to a plate, crush them with a fork to make a paste, and then stir the paste back into the sauce. Simmer for a few more minutes and add the basil leaves, then remove from the heat. Use immediately, or let cool and refrigerate for up to a week or freeze for up to 3 months.

FISH FUMET

Fish fumet (stock) only needs to simmer for 25 minutes, and as there's no need to skim off the fat, it can easily be prepared on the day of use. Avoid fish that are too fatty, such as salmon or mackerel, for this recipe, but shrimp, crayfish, and lobster heads and shells add a nice, slightly sweet taste.

2lbs (about 1kg) bones and heads of white-fleshed fish, gills removed

2 tablespoons olive oil

1 stalk celery, chopped

White of 1 small leek, washed and chopped

1/2 medium onion, chopped

1/4 fennel bulb, finely chopped

2 garlic cloves, peeled and sliced in half

1/2 cup (125ml) white wine

4 cups (1L) water

1/2 lemon, sliced

A few sprigs parsley

A few sprigs thyme

1 sprig rosemary

- Wash the fish bones and heads thoroughly under cold water.

- In a stockpot over medium heat, heat the olive oil and add the chopped vegetables and garlic. Sauté for a few minutes, until tender, then add the fish bones, heads, and wine. Cook for a few minutes, stirring occasionally, until the wine has reduced by half.

- Increase the heat to medium-high, pour in the water, and bring to a boil. Skim off any foam that accumulates on the surface. Add the lemon slices and herbs, reduce the heat to low, and simmer for 25 minutes. Strain the fumet through a fine sieve and let cool. Use immediately, or refrigerate for up to 1 day. You can also freeze the fumet for up to a month.

CARAMELIZED APPLESAUCE

MAKES 2 CUPS (500ML)

I never bother peeling my apples when making applesauce,
but go ahead and peel them if you wish.

4 apples, washed, cored, and sliced into small pieces

Juice of 1 lemon

1/3 cup (65g) sugar

3 tablespoons butter

2 tablespoons water

1/2 teaspoon ground cinnamon or 1 teaspoon vanilla

Pinch of salt

- Toss the apples with the lemon juice and set aside.

- Place the sugar in a medium pot over medium-high heat and cook until it melts and begins to color. Swirl the pot often to achieve a uniform caramel. Remove from the heat and then quickly stir in the butter, followed by the apples and the water. Place the pot back over medium-low heat, partially cover, and cook the mixture until the apples disintegrate, about 8 minutes.

- Stir in the cinnamon (or vanilla) and salt, remove from the heat, and let cool a bit. When it is still warm, purée in a blender until smooth. Store, refrigerated in a covered jar, for up to 3 days.

CHOCOLATE-COVERED BLUEBERRIES

MAKES ABOUT 45 CLUSTERS

A common sight in Quebec supermarkets and candy stores, chocolate-covered fruit, most often blueberries but also cranberries, were invented by Quebec Trappist monks in the 1960s. Making them at home is quite simple. Here is my recipe for success.

2 cups (about 340g) fresh blueberries, preferably high-bush (large) blueberries

3 cups (1lb/500g) chopped dark chocolate or chocolate buttons

1 tablespoon coconut oil

- Pick through the blueberries to remove any that are not intact. Wash quickly and pat dry with paper towels. Let them air-dry completely before proceeding. Prepare a parchment-lined baking sheet.

- Using a bain-marie or microwave, melt the chocolate in a medium bowl until just warm; remove from heat and stir in the coconut oil.

- Place the bowl on a damp kitchen towel (this will prevent it from slipping as you work) and drop the blueberries 3 at a time into the chocolate. Using a fork, turn them over to coat them completely, then fish them out and drop them onto the baking sheet in clusters of 3.

- When you've dipped them all, place the baking sheet in the refrigerator until the clusters are firm. Store in the refrigerator until serving.

Here is a list of stores where I shop for everything from kitchen equipment to ingredients to croissants.

For croissants:

Montrealers are spoiled with a plethora of croissant options, but for something extra special, I'd opt for the croissants from these three establishments. Light, buttery, and flaky as all get out, these are the croissants of which dreams are made. Slather heavily with jam and enjoy!

Hof Kelsten, 4524 St-Laurent Blvd. hofkelsten.com

Café Bazin, 380 Victoria Ave. cafebazin.com

Fous Desserts, 809 Laurier Ave. E. fousdesserts.com

For cakes and pastries:

Chef Stephanie Labelle's innovative cakes and pastries are made with a sophisticated palate of local ingredients. Her pastry boutique, Pâtisserie Rhubarbe, is now online, with cakes and pastries available by order, as well as savoury items and catered meals. Those looking for more homey fare are sure to love Cocoa Locale, where baker Reema Singh's cakes are not only beautiful, but made with the best ingredients (Valrhona chocolate!). Her cookies, spiced brownies, and pretty petal-topped cupcakes are a treat, and her layer cakes would be my choice for a birthday celebration.

Pâtisserie Rhubarbe, patisserierhubarbe.com

Cocoa Locale, 4807 Park Ave.

LENSKY
LENSKY

For a box of chocolates:

Try Les Chocolats de Chloé for hand-dipped bonbons made with Valrhona chocolate. Lecavalier Petrone sells exquisite molded chocolates hand-painted with colored cocoa butter, as well as wedding cakes, pastries, and cookies. Ernestine is a great bet for colorful chocolates with a retro feel.

Les Chocolats de Chloé, 546 Duluth Ave. E. leschocolatsdechloe.com
Lecavalier Petrone, 2423 Centre St. lecavalierpetrone.com
Ernestine, several sales points. ernestine.ca

For donuts:

Mile-End hotspot Bernie Beignes is a favorite for classics like glazed crullers, apple fritters, and jam-filled donuts handmade the traditional way. Across town is another fave, Homer's, in NDG for scrumptious traditional and deluxe donuts (try the Oreo). In St-Henri, head to Léché Desserts for donuts like Boston cream, lemon poppy seed, passion fruit, and simple cinnamon sugar.

Bernie Beignes, 23 Bernard St. W.
Homer's, 6206 Sherbrooke St W. homersmtl.ca
Léché Desserts, 640 Courcelle St. lechedesserts.com

For ice cream:

Crèmerie Dalla Rose is renowned for its vibrant and unusual ice cream flavors like coconut/chocolate swirl and Quebec corn. Kem Coba is famous for its delicious brown butter ice cream and strawberry cheesecake soft serve. Ripples is worth the detour, especially for their Chocolate 6X ice cream. And Havre aux Glaces is a must for its ice creams and sorbets, as well as its ice cream cakes and iced macarons.

LA MAISON DE
L'ORIGINAL
FAIRMOUNT
BAGEL
1950
1950
LA MAISON DE
L'ORIGINAL
FAIRMOUNT
BAGEL
FESTIVAL DE
FAIRMOUNT
BAGEL
100 ANS

Crèmerie Dalla Rose, 4609 Notre-Dame St. W. dallarose.ca
Kem Coba, 60 Fairmount Ave. W. kemcoba.com
Ripples, 3971 St-Laurent Blvd and 5554 Jeanne Mance St. ripplesicecream.com
Havre aux Glaces, 7070 Henri-Julien St. at the Jean-Talon Market. havreauxglaces.ca

For bagels:

The Fairmount and St-Viateur bagel shops are the city's most famous, and not just in Montreal, but—sorry, New Yorkers—in the world. Both shops are 24-hour operations, so half the fun is buying a dozen in the dead of the night. I'm also a fan of R.E.A.L. Bagel, where the bagels are bit more bready but equally delicious.

Fairmount Bagel, 74 Fairmount St. W. fairmountbagel.com
St-Viateur Bagel, 263 St-Viateur St. W. stviateurbagel.com
R.E.A.L. Bagel, 4940 Queen Mary Rd.

For bread:

For everything from baguettes to viennoiseries to quiche, try Autumne, where they not only craft the finest loaves but also mill their own flour. Miette Boulangerie makes the most delicious sourdough bread; their olive loaf alone is worth the trip to Little Burgundy. Le Toledo has won awards for its baguettes, but everything they make is wonderful. In Ahuntsic, try the original La Bête à Pain, which now has several locations around the city. La Meunerie Urbaine is the top spot in NDG, and Hof Kelsten is always a great bet, especially for panettone and challah.

Autumne, 6500 Christophe-Colomb Ave. automneboulangerie.com
Miette Boulangerie, 317 de Lévis St. mietteboulangerie.com
Le Toledo, 351 Mont-Royal Ave. E. and 4448 rue Wellington in Verdun. letoledo.com
La Bête à Pain, 114 Fleury St. W. and 195 Young St. labeteapain.com

La Meunerie Urbaine, 6151 Monkland Ave. in NDG. lameunerieurbaine.com
Hof Kelsten, 4524 St Laurent Blvd. hofkelsten.com

For cheese:

With hundreds of varieties of cheese, Quebec is Canada's cheese mecca, and with that reputation come several fantastic cheese shops. All of the ones listed below offer outstanding service as well as a wide selection of imported and local varieties, my favorites being the Bête à Seguin, Grey Owl, Zacharie Cloutier, Pied-de-Vent, and Alfred Le Fermier.

Yannick, 1218 Bernard St. W. in Outremont and 1001 Beaubien St. E.
yannickfromagerie.ca
Fromagerie Hamel, 138 Atwater Ave. at the Atwater Market, 220 Jean-Talon St. E. at
the Jean-Talon Market, and 2129 Mont-Royal Ave. E. fromageriehamel.com
Fromagerie du Marché Atwater, 134 Atwater Ave. at the Atwater Market, 1269
Ontario St. E. fromagerieatwater.ca

For fresh fish:

The preferred fishmonger of Montreal chefs, La Mer boasts the best selection of local and imported fish and seafood. All fish is sold fresh, on ice, in the refrigerated section of their shop, along with a great choice of lobster, oysters, smoked fish, caviar, and more. When I can't get to La Mer, I head to Falero, a smaller shop on Park Avenue with a fine selection of fresh and frozen specimens. Service is a bit gruff, but these guys know their stuff.

Poissonerie La Mer, 1840 René-Lévesque Blvd. E. lamer.ca
Poissonerie Nouveau Falero, 5726A Park Ave. falero.ca

For steak:

Owned by Marc Bourg, the most passionate butcher you will ever meet, Le Marchand de Bourg is not so much a butcher shop as a steak boutique specializing in steaks aged for at least 40 days and up to a year. A unique shop definitely worth a visit.

Le Marchand du Bourg, 1661 Beaubien St. E. marchanddubourg.com

For meat:

These are the butcher shops I visit most often and for very specific items: Chez Vito for veal, sausages, and Italian imports; Boucherie de Tours for offal, French cuts of meat, as well as goose and foie gras; Le Maître Boucher for marinated chickens; Latina for aged beef, poultry, and sausages; and Boucherie Atlantic, a German specialty store, for sausages, pork, and ham. Boucherie Lawrence and Boucherie Provisions are both restaurant offshoots with organic meats and an excellent choice of local products and produce.

Chez Vito, 5180 St-Urbain St.
Boucherie de Tours, 138 Atwater Ave. at the Atwater Market. boucheriedetours.ca
Le Maître Boucher, 5719 Monkland Ave. in NDG. lemaitreboucher.com
Latina, 185 St-Viateur St W. chezlatina.com
Boucherie Atlantic, 5060 Côte-des-Neiges Rd. boucherieatlantique.ca
Boucherie Lawrence, 5237 St-Laurent Blvd. boucherielawrence.com
Boucherie Provisions, 1142 Van Horne Ave. boucherieprovisions.ca

For fresh produce:

In addition to our fabulous public markets, Chez Nino is where chefs, food stylists, TV cooks, and more head for the freshest fruit and vegetables, local and imported. Faves include their amazing array of citrus fruit and wild arugula. For locally grown produce, you can't do better than La Ferme des Quatre-Temps. Run by famous organic gardener Jean-Martin Fortier, this farm has a stand at the Jean-Talon Market but also offers locations around the city for drop-offs of their eggs, vegetables, meats, and more.

Chez Nino, 192 Pl. du Marché-du-Nord at the Jean-Talon Market.
La Ferme des Quatre-Temps, 7070 Henri-Julien Ave. at the Jean-Talon Market.
fermequatretemps.com

For wild edibles:

Run by chef Nancy Hinton and her partner, famed forager François Brouillard, this popular kiosk at the Jean-Talon Market offers an impressive array of local wild edibles, especially wild mushrooms. You'll also find preserved and dried wild edibles, as well as seasoned salts, spices, soups, and prepared meals.

Les Jardins Sauvages, 7070 Henri-Julien Ave. at the Jean-Talon Market.
jardinssauvages.com

For gourmet products:

In search of gourmet vinegars, French chocolate bars, or British cheese biscuits? Look no further than these three amazing shops, which carry a huge array of imported—particularly French and Italian—products.

Gourmet Laurier, 1042 Laurier Ave. W. gourmetlaurier.ca
Les Douceurs du Marché, 138 Atwater Ave. at the Atwater Market.
lesdouceursdumarche.ca
Le Fouvrac Fleury, 1404 rue Fleury E. fouvrac.com

For Québécois products:

A one-stop shop for those looking for the best Québécois products, Le Marché des Saveurs carries an extensive selection of maple syrups and maple products, condiments, tisanes, cranberries, frozen meats, prepared meals, and wines. Their cheese counter features an unmatched selection of local cheeses. Comptoir Sainte-Cécile is a hybrid grocery store/casual restaurant offering sandwiches, brunch, and take-out meals near the Jean-Talon Market. You'll also find a good selection of Québécois products, most especially local wines, ciders, and beers.

Le Marché des Saveurs du Québec, 280 Pl. du Marché-du-Nord at the Jean-Talon Market. Comptoir Sainte-Cécile, 232 rue de Castelnau St. E.

For tea:

Camellia Sinensis has legions of fans who flock to their tea shops to taste and buy the freshest and best teas on the planet. How great are their teas? When it comes to Darjeelings alone, co-owner Kevin Gascoyne heads out on month-long tea-buying treks to the Himalayas above Darjeeling. Of the approximately 300 teas he samples, only a dozen make the cut. Get the picture? Look also for oolongs, white teas, green teas, Quebec tisanes, and more.

Camellia Sinensis, 351 Emery St. and 7010 Casgrain Ave. camellia-sinensis.com

For coffee:

Café Union is a Montreal institution where you can buy single origin coffee or blends. Prices are reasonable, and you can also pick up espresso machines, grinders, and coffee accessories on-site. Café in Gamba is a great spot for a wide selection of imported Third Wave beans, and you get a free coffee with every purchase. If you're looking for Third Wave–style coffee roasted right in the city, St-Henri is your best bet.

Café Union, 148 Jean-Talon St. W. cafeunion.com
Café in Gamba, 5263 Park Ave. and 71 St-Viateur St. cafeingamba.com
St-Henri, 7335 Mile-End St. and 3632 Notre-Dame W. sainthenri.ca

For pots, pans, and other kitchen equipment:

When I need basic kitchenware from jam jars to Le Creuset pots to a hand-cranked pasta machine, Quincaillerie Dante, run by the amazing Elena Faita, is my go-to. Prices are fair and the staff provides terrific advice and service. For more professional grade goods, try Tzanet Restaurant Equipment, where you can find chef's knives, large cookie sheets, storage bins, tart molds, and nonstick frying pans. For European-style cookware, Staub pots, and baking accessories, I recommend Boutique Crème, which also offers cooking classes (sometimes by me!).

Quincaillerie Dante, 6851 St-Dominique St. quincailleriedante.com
Tzanet, 1375 De Louvain st. W. tzanet.com
Boutique Crème, 152 Laurier Ave. W. boutique1101.com

For cookbooks:

Besides the regular chain stores, these two shops sell a wide selection of cookbooks and cooking magazines, including the latest releases, classics, and hard-to-find European imports. Appetite for Books specializes in English books, whereas Librairie Gourmande puts the emphasis on French texts. Ask about the cooking classes too at Appetite for Books (many with a cookbook theme). The Librairie Gourmande also sells plenty of kitchen gadgets.

Appetite for Books, 388 Victoria Ave. in Westmount. appetitebooks.ca
Librairie Gourmande, 7070 Henri Julien Ave. at the Jean-Talon Market.

For Dining Out

These are the restaurants I recommend on a regular basis for both casual and fancy nights out.

For late-night eats:

Chances are if you're looking for food at 3 a.m., you need something to pick you up post-partying. What could be better than a heaping plate of poutine? With more than 30 types to choose from at La Banquise, there's something for everyone. It's open 24 hours a day, but expect a line at most times. And it's an excellent choice for eating with kids too. You will also find poutine at the iconic Gibeau Orange Julep, better known as the big orange dome on the Décarie Expressway, but the real draws here are the hot dogs and the mysterious frothy orange drink. Open until 4 a.m., Orange Julep is a destination no local or visitor should pass up.

La Banquise, 994 Rachel St. E. labanquise.com
Gibeau Orange Julep, 7700 Décarie Blvd. orangejulep.ca

Best spot for natural wines:

Montreal is known as a hotspot for natural wines and there are many bars and restaurants serving these sometimes weird and often wonderful vinos. I chose these three excellent restaurants specifically for the women behind their wine selections: at Foxy, the phenomenal Véronique Dalle; at Mon Lapin, the famous Vanya Filipovic; and at Alma, the charming Lindsay Brennan.

Foxy, 1638 Notre-Dame St. W. foxy.restaurant/info
Mon Lapin, 150 Saint-Zotique St. E. vinmonlapin.com
Alma, 1231 Lajoie Ave. in Outremont. almamontreal.com

Best for swanky sushi:

Montreal's sushi scene is not huge, but these two restaurants are standouts for raw fish aficionados. Named for its chef Antonio Park, Park is renowned for its new-style sushi with influences from the chef's Korean and Argentinian heritage. At Jun I, the style is more classic but equally exquisite. For an extra-special experience, be sure to book a seat at the sushi bar at either restaurant. And remember, good sushi comes at a high price.

Park, 378 Victoria Ave. parkresto.com
Jun I, 156 Laurier Ave. juni.ca

Best for French fries:

You can find plenty of great fries in Montreal, but on the restaurant scene, my top spot goes to Leméac, for their thin, crisp, and scrumptious frites, most often served with mussels or their famous hanger steak. On the more casual front are the fries at Frite Alors, a small chain with several locations around the city, where the fries are served in cornets with a selection of flavored mayos alongside. Seriously delicious and a smart choice for kids.

Leméac, 1045 Laurier Ave. W. in Outremont. restaurantlemeac.com
Frite Alors, several locations around the city. fritealors.com

Best deli for smoked meat:

Montrealers constantly debate smoked meat preferences, and I cannot deny that my top pick is not the favorite, Schwartz's Deli (the oldest deli in Canada and still fabulous), but the lesser-known Snowdon Deli, because their smoked meat sandwich is so juicy and the restaurant, in operation since 1946, has such an old-world feel. Of course, Schwartz's smoked meat is also superb, and lunch at their counter (with a cherry cola and a plate of half-sour pickles) is one of Montreal life's great experiences.

Schwartz's, Montreal

Schwartz's Deli, 3895 St-Laurent Blvd. schwartzsdeli.com
Snowdon Deli, 5265 Decarie Blvd. snowdondeli.com

Best for posh poutine:

Poutine is now a Canadian favorite, but I like two versions that present this Québécois original in an innovative way. First at Ma Poule Mouillée, where a classic poutine is enhanced with another Montreal fave, Portuguese rotisserie chicken. And second is the famous foie gras poutine from Au Pied de Cochon, where the poutine is topped with slabs of seared foie gras and doused with a foie gras–enhanced sauce. Yum!

Ma Poule Mouillée, 969 Rachel St E. mapoulemouillee.ca
Au Pied de Cochon, 536 Av. Duluth E. aupieddecochon.ca

Best for hamburgers:

There are plenty of great burgers in Montreal, but the ones I go back to repeatedly are the smash burgers from Chez Tousignant, served on their homemade potato buns. When I want a burger with wine, I'll head to Nouveau Palais, where you can enjoy a great burger and fries with a well-priced organic wine to match.

Chez Tousignant, 6956 Drolet St. cheztousignant.com
Nouveau Palais, 281 Bernard St. W. nouveaupalais.com

Best for a true taste of the city:

Montreal is known not only for its great food and a strong wine scene, but also for its joie de vivre. Dining out in Montreal means that you are not only going to eat well, you will have a wonderful time. At Montreal Plaza, the room is stunning, the food is amazing, the staff is solicitous, and the ambiance is electric. At Au Pied de Cochon, the bacchanalian atmosphere and the Nouvelle-Québécois cuisine is always fun, and the cool staff certainly keeps the good times rolling. Le Filet is the choice for a night of delicious small plates and amazing people watching, as it draws some of the city's most stylish diners. Joe Beef has become a destination for both regulars and, especially, affluent tourists eager to sample signature dishes like the foie gras terrine and lobster spaghetti, as well as terrific Canadian seafood. Le Club Chasse et Pêche is probably the city's most sophisticated eating establishment, with chic décor and innovative menu. Tavern on the Square is very anglo Montreal (très Westmount), and a bit clubby, but always welcoming, with perfect comfort food and outstanding wines.

Montreal Plaza, 6230 St-Hubert St. montrealplaza.com

Au Pied de Cochon, 536 Duluth Ave. E. aupieddecochon.ca

Le Filet, 219 Mont-Royal Ave W. lefilet.ca

Joe Beef, 2491 Notre-Dame St. W. joebeef.com

Le Club Chasse et Pêche, 423 Saint-Claude St. leclubchasseetpeche.com

Tavern on the Square, 1 Westmount Sq. in Westmount. tavernonthesquare.ca

For the new generation of star chefs:

Those who crave an "haute" experience delivered by the city's newest generation of chefs are sure to relish these four restaurants. First, Le Mousso, whose chef-owner Antonin Mousseau-Rivard is considered Montreal's top culinary *artiste*. A night here is pricey, but this is gastronomy of the highest order complete with the best local produce. Sabayon is run by the husband-wife team of chef Patrice Demers and maître d'/sommelier Marie-Josée Beaudoin. They serve a divine set tasting menu, but the restaurant is small, so reservations are hard to come by. Happily, they serve afternoon tea as well, so try to nab a table for either service. Mastard is the brainchild of chef Simon Mathys, arguably Montreal's most under-the-radar gastronomic star. His food is Michelin-star perfection and the service at the unpretentious resto is top-notch. For those up for something more casual but still superb, try chef Marc-Olivier Frappier's newest restaurant, Rôtisserie La Lune. Frappier and his wife Vanya Filipovic made their name with the nearby Mon Lapin and at this, their second restaurant, chicken is the star of the show. Sommelier Filipovic has curated a wine list to take their beautiful birds from a casual to a fine-dining adventure.

Le Mousso, 1025 Ontario Street E. lemousso.com
Sabayon 2194 Rue Centre, Pointe-Saint-Charles sabayon.ca
Mastard 1879 rue Bélanger St. E. restaurantmastard.com
Rôtisserie La Lune, 391 Saint-Zotique St. E. rotisserielalune.com

Best for catching up with a friend over coffee:

Wildly popular from the day it opened in Old Montreal in 1998, Olive and Gourmando has been *the* spot for hip locals and visiting celebrities ever since. Everything from the salads to the baked goods to soups and sandwiches is of the highest quality. It's a bit pricey but totally worth it. The little sister of the East End restaurant Hélicoptère, Hélico features divine pastries, superb Third Wave coffee, soups, sandwiches, and even oysters and fine wines. The café is small, so in warm weather, grab a spot on their terrace or opt for take-out to enjoy while strolling through the Maisonneuve Market a block away.

Olive and Gourmando, 351 St-Paul St. W. oliveetgourmando.com
Hélico, 2009 de la Salle Ave. helicopteremtl.com

Best place to catch up with a friend over a beer:

Both of these fab restaurants brew their own (excellent) beer on-site, and both serve fabulous food. My choices at Harricana are the amazing hamburger, the lobster roll, and the carrot cake. At Reservoir, the beer-friendly food is served in the small-plate format, and there's a fine selection of wines, ciders, and cocktails.

Brasserie Harricana, 95 Jean-Talon St. W. brasserieharricana.com
Reservoir Brasseur, 9 Duluth Ave. E. reservoirbrasseur.com

Best for pizza:

Excellent pizzerias abound in Montreal, but I'd begin with Bottega, the pizzeria that got the Naples-style–pizza craze underway in the city. Side dishes are a hit as well, and there is a superb wine list. Just across the street, smack in the middle of Little Italy, is Pizzeria Gema, where the pepperoni is homemade, the pizza is drop dead delicious, and the wine list is full of organic Italian vinos. Don't skip the frozen custard desserts. Melrose is a wildly popular neighborhood restaurant offering half a dozen starters and 10 pizzas, with a few daily specials worth exploring. I also enjoy Pizzeria 900, a Montreal-wide chain where the prices are reasonable, the Neapolitan pizzas are gorgeous, and the wine selection is made up entirely of organic bottles, many from Quebec!

Bottega, 65 St-Zotique St. E. bottega.ca
Gema Pizzeria, 6827 St-Dominique St. pizzeriagema.com
Pizzeria Melrose, 5779 Sherbrooke St W. pizzeriamelrose.com
Pizzeria 900, with locations throughout the city. no900.com

Best for Italian:

Located in the heart of Montreal's Little Italy, Impasto is the ideal spot to enjoy modern Italian cuisine that doesn't stray too far from nonna's kitchen. Everything from charcuterie to pasta to desserts is homemade, and the quality of the ingredients and service is superb. Equally impressive is the Old Montreal favorite Graziella, where chef Graziella Battista serves some of the most sophisticated Italian cuisine in the city. Two newer establishments, Moccione and Antoinetta, in the east of the city, offer fabulous food in a relaxed setting. Both are popular, so book well in advance.

Impasto, 48 Dante St. impastomtl.ca

Graziella, 116 McGill St. restaurantgraziella.ca

Moccione, 7495 St-Denis St. moccione.com

Antoinetta, 6672 Papineau Ave. antonietta.ca

Best for a business dinner or lunch:

Located right downtown, Ferreira is an elegant Portuguese restaurant where the business crowd comes to cut deals over grilled sardines, fresh fish, fine wines, and rare ports. The lunch special is a deal, and for the best people watching, request a seat on the main floor. Toqué! is often considered the city's top gourmet spot, so for a fancy dinner or formal lunch, it is another sure bet for business types (especially as the tables are well spaced). Montreal's most beautiful restaurant, Monarque, is divided into a brasserie space up front and a quieter restaurant behind. The food is terrific, as is the service. In summer, Maison Boulud is a winner when your quest is to impress. Ask for a table in the garden, where you can admire the ducks while enjoying star chef Daniel Boulud's French/Italian menu. Be prepared: all these restos will set you back a pretty penny.

Ferreira Café, 1446 Peel St. ferreiracafe.com

Toqué!, 900 place Jean-Paul-Riopelle. restaurant-toque.com

Monarque, 406 Saint-Jacques St. restaurantmonarque.ca

Maison Boulud, 1228 Sherbrooke St. W. in the Ritz-Carlton Hotel. maisonboulud.com

Best place for a dating app date:

With two locations, Satay Brothers is the perfect place to meet up for a blind date. I would especially recommend their stand at the Atwater Market in summer, as the excellent Singaporean street food will give you plenty to talk about (order the papaya salad and see who finds it too spicy), and there is a metro nearby if you need to make a quick getaway. For a fancier date, I'd opt for Île

Flottante, a Plateau restaurant renowned for its beautiful tasting menus. It's expensive, so best for the passionate foodies.

Satay Brothers, 3721 Notre-Dame St. W. and at the stand at Atwater Market.
sataybrothers.com
Île Flottante, 176 Saint-Viateur W. restaurantileflottante.com

Best for dining solo at the bar:

When I'm dining alone, restaurant bar seating is my first choice. My favored stools are at the Outremont bistro Leméac, where the bar is filled with locals, professionals, and shoppers eating steak frites and drinking Pinot Noir. At L'Express, the bar is a preferred spot for regulars, day, night, and until the wee hours in the morning. (They close at 1 a.m.) Then there's Au Pied de Cochon, where the bar seating faces the open kitchen, and where tourists sit elbow to elbow with locals happy to watch the action unfold—and there's plenty of it. And if you're a serious gourmet, up for a tasting menu that's sure to impress, book a bar seat at Lawrence to soak up the magical cooking of chef Marc Cohen. These spots are coveted, so make sure to book well in advance, but it's also always worth showing up unannounced to snag a last-minute seat at the bar.

Leméac, 1045 Laurier Ave. W. in Outremont. restaurantlemeac.com
L'Express, 3927 St-Denis St. restaurantlexpress.com
Au Pied de Cochon, 536 Duluth Ave. E. aupieddecochon.ca
Lawrence, 9 Fairmount Ave. E. lawrencemtl.com

L'Express, Montreal

ACKNOWLEDGMENTS

At Simon & Schuster Canada, thanks to Kevin Hanson, Nicole Winstanley, and my editors, Kirsten Hanson, Grace O'Connell, and Judith Sutton.

Thanks also to the team at Les Éditions Cardinal, especially director Antoine Ross-Trempe and editor Joëlle Landry.

This book is a beauty thanks to photographer (and gourmand!) Maude Chauvin and prop stylist (the incomparable) Daniel Raiche. Kitchen assistant Marie-Christine Champagne made every dish better than I ever could have. Book designer Catherine Gravel brought her vision and taste to this project every day of the shoot and beyond. Big thanks as well to the Simon & Schuster design team who did a spectacular job.

Thanks to all the chefs who generously allowed me to share their recipes in these pages.

An extra special thank-you to my sons, Max and Luke Bazin, who always gave me an honest opinion on what they ate, and their dad, Bertrand Bazin, for the never-ending pastry advice.

Thanks to my Toronto posse, Naomi Duguid, Dawn Woodward, Laura Calder, and Jennifer MacLagan.

To my sister, Lorraine Holl, for her love and excellent advice, and to my main man, Jean Aubry, for . . . everything.

I must also thank all the great restaurateurs, chefs, pastry chefs, sous-chefs, commis, maitre d's, sommeliers, waiters, busboys, and dishwashers, not to mention the farmers, butchers, cheese makers, and other food suppliers, who have made Montreal one of the world's great food cities.

And, finally, to my readers and listeners from over 30 years in the food media in Quebec and Canada: Thanks! Or, as we say here in Quebec, MERCI!

INDEX

Note: Page references in *italics* indicate photographs.